Women Around the Messenger

COMPANIONS OF THE
PROPHET ﷺ SERIES

Women Around the Messenger

COMPANIONS OF THE PROPHET ﷺ SERIES

Khalid Muhammed Khalid

1 2 3 4 5 6 7 8 9 10

All rights reserved. No part of this publication may be reproduced, stored in a retrieval system or transmitted in any form or by any means – electronic, mechanical, photocopying, recording or otherwise – without written permission from the publisher.

© Light Publishing 2015

Khalid Muhammed Khalid

Women Around the Messenger

ISBN 978-1-915570-03-1

www.lightpublishing.co.uk

بسم الله الرحمن الرحيم

CONTENTS

INTRODUCTION 11

THE MOTHERS 13
   Amina bint Wahb 13
   Thuwayba 15
   Baraka 15
   Halima bint Abi Dhu'ayb 19
   Fatima bint Asad 22

MOTHERS OF THE BELIEVERS 25
   Khadija bint Khuwaylid 25
   Sawda bint Zama 30
   Aisha bint Abu Bakr 32
   Hafsa bint Umar 40
   Zaynab bint Khuzayma 43
   Umm Salama 44
   Umm Habiba Ramla bint Abu Sufyan 51
   Zaynab bint Jahsh 55
   Safiya bint Huyay 58
   Juwayriyya bint al-Harith 61
   Maymuna bint al-Harith 64
   Maria al-Qibtbiya 67

MUHAMMAD, THE HUSBAND 73
    The Good-Humoured Husband 74
    The Serious Husband 75
    The Faithful Husband 76

THE PROPHET'S DAUGHTERS 79
    Zaynab 79
    Ruqayya 83
    Umm Kulthum 86
    Fatima al-Zahra 89

THE COMPANIONS 99
    Khawla bint Hakim 99
    Asma bint Abu Bakr 101
    Fatima bint al-Khattab 106
    Umm Kulthum bint Ali ibn Abu Talib 108
    Safiya bint Abdul Muttalib 110
    Sumaya bint Khayyat 112
    Asma bint Yazid ibn al-Sakan 113
    Umm Sulaym bint Malhan 114
    Umm Haram bint Malhan 119
    Umm Waraqa 120
    Asma bint Umays 121
    Al-Shifa bint Abdullah 124
    Umm Hakim bint al-Harith 125
    Hind bint Utbah 127
    Umm Sharik 129
    Umm al-Fadl 130
    Al-Rubai bint Muawidh 132
    Al-Khansa 133

Khawla bint Thaalaba	135
Umm Romaan	137
Nussaibah bint Ka'ab (Umm Amara)	138
Umm Mihjan	141
Umm Hani and Nab'a	142
Umm Ma'bad and Naba	143
Rufayda al-Aslamiya	145
Umm Kulthum bint Uqba	146
Umm Mani	147
Shayma bint Harith	148
Khawla bint al-Azwar	149
Zunairah al-Rumiya	151
Hamna bint Jahsh	151

INTRODUCTION

Praise be to Allah, Lord of the Worlds, and peace and blessings be upon the final Messenger of Allah, his household, his Companions and those who follow his guidance.

Every day, Muslims in all corners of the earth make supplications, send peace and ask of Allah's pleasure for the *sahaba* of our blessed Prophet Muhammad ﷺ. While much emphasis is given to the noble men who supported, learned from and loved the Prophet ﷺ, it is equally crucial to give due respect to his female companions.

The women around Prophet Muhammad ﷺ were all uniquely exceptional human beings who have gifted us with a rich legacy of wisdom, courage and steadfastness of belief. There were those who gave all they had for the cause of Allah, who risked their lives in the face of persecution and who spread the beauty and radiance of Islam.

It is through the account of these Companions, that we are able to magnify the light of love for our Prophet Muhammad ﷺ and to deepen the belief in our hearts. This book aims to provide intimate glimpses into the lives and characters of these extraordinary women, who lived and breathed around the best of teachers, Prophet Muhammad ﷺ. The Companions witnessed with their own eyes all of his ﷺ virtues and noble characteristics. They observed his chastity, his purity, his honesty, his integrity, his eloquence and his courage ﷺ. The Companions measured their conduct and behaviour through their vision and perception of his ﷺ truth, goodness and beauty. Prophet Muhammad ﷺ was his community's conscience, and he found comfort and company in his fellow believers.

The women around the Messenger ﷺ were his pillars of support, his protectors and his confidants. The first person to believe in the Prophet ﷺ

was the noble Lady Khadija ﷺ, who was as firm as a mountain by his side. She encouraged him, lifted him and strengthened him through the most challenging and crucial part of his mission. The Prophet ﷺ said of Khadija, "She believed in me when no one else did. She accepted Islam when people rejected me. She comforted me and supported me when people denied me."

There were the mother figures of the Prophet ﷺ who tenderly nurtured him from his infancy, like Halima, his Bedouin wet nurse who poured milk into his blessed veins. Never forgetting the ones who cared for him, years later Halima visited him in Medina, and he rose to receive her with honour, exclaiming, "My mother, my mother!"

There was also Umm Amara, the warrior woman who defended the Prophet ﷺ so valiantly against the enemy attack in the battle of Uhud that the Prophet ﷺ said whatever direction his face turned on the battlefield, he saw Umm Amara there to defend him.

There were also great scholars like Umm Waraqa, expert medical practitioners like Rufayda al-Aslamiya and, of course, above all, the exemplary and inspirational wives and daughters of the Prophet ﷺ.

In the pages of this book, we will lay out the lives of these noble female Companions who stood in the light of Muhammad, the Messenger of Allah ﷺ, and who themselves became a beacon for Muslims throughout the centuries.

Khalid Muhammad Khalid

THE MOTHERS

AMINA BINT WAHB

Amina bint Wahb was one of the most eminent women of the Quraysh. Her parents were distant cousins from a noble Quraysh family. Her father was Wahb bin 'Abd Manaf, chief of the Banu Zuhra, and her was mother, Barra bint Abd al-Uzza. After the death of her father, Amina was placed under the guardianship of his successor and her uncle, Wuhayb bin Abd Manaf.

As a young woman of such prestige and lineage, Amina was much sought after in marriage. Abdul Muttalib, who was a man respected and honoured for his generosity and integrity by the Quraysh, considered Amina as the only potential bride for his cherished son, Abdullah – the son he had previously vowed to sacrifice, but who was ransomed from slaughtering.

Abdullah was a twenty-five-year-old man of high morals and good, sociable character. He was so handsome that he was known as the Yusuf of his time. He had the light of radiance shining from his face. It was the light of prophethood that would leave him and take seed in Amina's womb.

Amina and Abdallah's marriage was very happy, but it was short-lived. Abdullah was to join a trade caravan that was leaving for Syria. Amina was reluctant to be parted from her husband so soon into the marriage, even more so as she was expecting a child, but she knew Abdul Muttalib wished for his son to go. Abdullah was never to see his bride again. He contracted a disease on the return journey and died in Yathrib, later known as Medina.

Amina was utterly devastated. She wept and wailed bitterly. Abdul Muttalib, who was also heartbroken, never left her side. He constantly comforted and cared for his young, widowed daughter-in-law.

But Amina was carrying a light within her womb – it contained the seal of all the prophets and the leader of all the messengers. She dreamt that a man came to her and told her, "You are pregnant with the leader and the prophet of this *ummah*." He came to her again before she gave birth and told her, "After you have delivered him say, 'I seek protection for him with the One, from the evil of every jealous person.' Then name him Muhammad. "

Amina's dreams continued. They gave her strength, patience and joy for the child she was carrying. It's said that she had an easy pregnancy and never faced any discomfort or sickness. Even the delivery was smooth and easy. Her child was born at dawn on the twelfth day of Rabi al-Awwal.

Amina was reported to have said, "When I delivered him, a light came out with him that illuminated what is between the East and the West. The light illuminated palaces and markets of Syria until I saw the necks of the camels in Basra. I saw three erected flags: one at the East, one at the West and the third over the Kaaba."

Abdul Muttalib took the baby to the Kaaba, joyously circling it and saying, "Praise be to Allah Who gave me this greatly important boy. I seek Allah's protection for him."

When he returned the baby to his mother, Amina told Abdul Muttalib about the voices who instructed her to call her son Muhammad, meaning "often praised" or "worthy of praise".

As was custom for the noble families at the time, the infant Muhammad ﷺ was sent to the desert to be suckled by a Bedouin wet nurse. After a few years, Muhammad ﷺ was returned to Amina, and she doted on her beloved son. She never remarried after her husband's death, even though it was commonplace for widows to remarry, but she filled her days with her son and wanted for nothing more than his company. When Muhammad ﷺ was six years old, Amina decided to take her young son to Yathrib (later called Medina) to visit her relatives. They had stayed there for a month before making the journey back to Mecca. But the sad fate that befell her husband, Abdullah, was also written for Amina. She fell extremely ill and died on the return journey in the village of Abwa, not far from Yathrib. Muhammad's heart was filled with grief and sorrow. Until his last days, he never forgot his beloved mother, Amina, mother of the final messenger ﷺ.

THUWAYBA

Thuwayba was the very first wet nurse of the blessed Prophet Muhammad ﷺ. She was a slave girl of Muhammad's uncle, Abu Lahab, who was brother to Muhammad's recently deceased father, Abdullah. As soon as she heard of the birth of Amina's child, Thuwayba went running to her master with the happy news. Abu Lahab was so overcome with joy that he freed her there and then. He gestured with his thumb and forefinger, saying to Thuwayba, "Go, for you are free."

It is said that when Abu Lahab died in disbelief, a relative (possibly Abbas) saw him in a dream in the most wretched of conditions, and said to him, "What did you find [after death]?" So Abu Lahab replied, "I didn't find [any rest] since I left you all, except that I was given to drink this little amount because of my freeing Thuwayba." (Bukhari, Saheeh)

Thuwayba stayed with Amina for a few days to nurse the Prophet ﷺ until a long-term wet-nurse could be found. Thuwayba had just given birth herself to a son called Masruh and lovingly suckled the two boys. Thuwayba had also nursed the Prophet's uncle, Hamza, and Abu Salama, son of Barrah bint Abdul-Mutallib, who was the Prophet's aunt.

The Prophet ﷺ always felt the deepest respect and love for his first milk-mother, Thuwayba, and he never forgot her. When he conquered Mecca sixty years later, he asked for her but learnt that she died a few years prior. Saddened by the news, he ﷺ then asked for Thuwayba's son, hoping to extend his kindness to his foster brother, but learned that he had also died before his mother.

Thuwayba ؓ was among the first to accept Islam when Muhammad ﷺ received his prophethood. She had the honour of gaining the love of the Prophet ﷺ and of giving him the first taste of milk in his life. Her name aptly means, 'Deserving of God's reward'. She died in 7 AH, may Allah have mercy on the Prophet's very first wet nurse.

BARAKA

Baraka was a young Abyssinian slave girl who the Prophet's father, Abdullah, saw being sold in the marketplace of Mecca. He had a generous heart and brought her back to become the only servant in his household, where he treated her with kindness. When Amina entered the home as a bride, Baraka looked after her new mistress with the greatest care and affection.

Soon after the marriage, when Amina was shaken to the core on hearing the tragic news of her husband's death, it was Baraka who was her stalwart rock of support. Baraka relates,

> Amina heard the painful news, she fainted, and I stayed by her bedside while she was in a state between life and death. There was no one else but me in Amina's house. I nursed her and looked after her during the day and through the long nights until she gave birth to her child Muhammad on a night in which the heavens were resplendent with the light of God.

When Amina gave birth, Baraka was the first to cradle the baby Muhammad ﷺ in her arms.

Years later, when Muhammad ﷺ returned from being weaned in the desert, Baraka joyfully welcomed him back into her embrace.

Baraka accompanied Amina on her journey to Yathrib. They went on two camels with Amina riding one and Baraka riding the other, while holding on to the blessed six-year-old Muhammad ﷺ. When Amina suddenly died, Baraka did everything she could to console the young boy. She knew how deeply he loved his mother and understood how alone he must have felt, now that he was an orphan for a second time.

Baraka returned with Muhammad ﷺ to Mecca and took him to his grandfather's house, where she stayed to care for him. Abdul Muttalib once told her, "Baraka, be mindful of my son for I had seen him with children near the lotus tree. The people of the Scripture are saying that my son is the prophet of this generation."

Baraka knew in her heart that Muhammad ﷺ was special. When she was in Medina with Amina and Muhammad ﷺ, she said,

> Two men from the Jews of Medina came to me one day and they told me, "Bring out for us Ahmad so that we can see him." They then looked at him and scrutinised him. One of them told his companion, "This is the prophet of this *ummah* and that is the place of his migration [referring to Medina]. There will be many killings and captives taken there."

When Abdul Muttalib died two years later, she took Muhammad ﷺ to his uncle Abu Talib's house and continued to look after him into adulthood, when he ﷺ married Lady Khadija.

And even then, Baraka stayed in Khadija's house with the married couple, as the bond between Baraka and the Prophet ﷺ was so strong. She once said, "I never left him and he never left me." One day Muhammad ﷺ called out to Baraka saying, "O mother! Now I am a married man, and you are still unmarried. What do you think if someone should come now and ask to marry you?" Baraka looked at Muhammad ﷺ and said, "I shall never leave you. Does a mother abandon her son?" Muhammad ﷺ smiled and kissed her head. He looked at his wife Khadija and said to her, "This is Baraka. This is my mother after my own mother. She is the rest of my family."

The Lady Khadija said to her, "Baraka, you have sacrificed your youth for the sake of Muhammad. Now he wants to return some of his obligations to you. For my sake and his, agree to be married before old age overtakes you." They suggested Ubayd ibn Zayd from the Khazraj tribe of Yathrib, and Baraka agreed and went to live in Yathrib where she gave birth to a son called Ayman, earning her the title of Umm Ayman. Her marriage, however, did not last long as her husband died, and so she returned to live with Muhammad ﷺ.

When Muhammad ﷺ received his prophethood, Baraka was among the first to accept Islam. Now as a Muslim, she faced great difficulty and danger. One night the hypocrites had blocked off the roads leading to the House of Arqam, where the Prophet ﷺ gathered his Companions regularly to teach them about Islam. Baraka had some urgent information from Khadija which had to be conveyed to the Prophet ﷺ, and she risked her life trying to reach the House of Arqam. When the Prophet ﷺ saw her, he knew the terrible risk she was taking in going to him. He smiled and said to her, "You are blessed, Umm Ayman. Surely you have a place in Paradise."

When Umm Ayman left, the Prophet ﷺ turned to his Companions and asked, "Should one of you desire to marry a woman from the people of Paradise, let him marry Umm Ayman."

The Companions remained silent. Umm Ayman was around 50 years old and plain looking. But then, Zayd ibn al-Harithah came forward and said, "Messenger of Allah, I shall marry Umm Ayman. By Allah, she is better than women who have grace and beauty." The Prophet ﷺ was elated that Zayd ibn al-Haritha, whom he loved deeply, would marry his beloved mother figure.

The marriage between Zayd and Umm Ayman took place and they were blessed with a son whom they named Usama. The Prophet ﷺ loved Usama like he was his own son. He would often play with him, kiss him and feed him with his own hands. His companions would affectionately say of Usama, "He is the beloved son of the Beloved."

When the Prophet ﷺ migrated to Yathrib, which was henceforth to be called Medina, he left Umm Ayman behind in Mecca to look after some special affairs in his household. She later migrated to Medina on her own, making the long and arduous journey through the desert and mountainous terrain on foot. She marched on, through the penetrating heat and sandstorms. When she reached Medina, her feet were sore and swollen and her face was covered with sand and dust. "*Ya* Umm Ayman! *Ya* Ummi!" ("O Umm Ayman! O my mother!") the Prophet ﷺ exclaimed, "Truly, for you is a place in Paradise!"

Umm Ayman played an active role in the Muslim community. At the Battle of Uhud she distributed water to the thirsty and tended to the wounded. She even accompanied the Prophet ﷺ on some of his expeditions to Khaybar and Hunayn.

Baraka's house was one of the few houses in which the Prophet ﷺ sought refreshment and rest. She would offer him his favourite food and he would enquire after her health and wellbeing, never forgetting the love and compassion she showed him as a child, as well as now, as a grown man. Whenever the Prophet ﷺ visited, her friends, the other female Companions, would be present, and always cherished the honour and blessings of his company.

Baraka lost her own dear son Ayman in battle. She was about seventy years old and quite frail, so she spent much of her time at home. The Prophet ﷺ, accompanied by Abu Bakr and Umar, often visited her. The Prophet ﷺ would ask, "Ya Ummi! Are you well?" Baraka would reply, "I am well, O Messenger of Allah, as long as Islam is."

Towards the end of her life, there were two occasions that tears would not leave Umm Ayman's eyes. The first was when the beloved Prophet ﷺ died and a light left her heart. Abu Bakr and Umar ﷺ knew of her deep grief and went to console her, knowing how close she had been to the Messenger of Allah ﷺ. Abu Bakr said to Umar, "Let us go and visit Umm Ayman as the Messenger of Allah used to do." When they entered her house, she again began to cry and they asked her, "Why are you crying? What is with Allah is better for His Messenger." Umm Ayman replied, "I am crying because the revelation from the heaven has stopped." Abu Bakr and Umar began to weep, and they shared tears together in their grief.

The second occasion on which Baraka cried was when Umar was martyred while he was standing in prayer. She cried so much that people became concerned and asked her why she shed so many tears. She said, "Today, Islam has been weakened." Baraka was a woman of great insight; she knew that Umar was a unique man under whose leadership the word of Islam had spread far and wide.

Umm Ayman lived a long life of profound faith that spanned decades. Baraka was the only person who knew the Prophet ﷺ from the second of his birth until his death. The deep bond between Baraka and Muhammad ﷺ meant they were close until the end of his life. The Prophet ﷺ held great love and deep respect for Baraka and her love for him was unshakeable until her final breath during the caliphate of Uthman ﷺ. May Allah bless Baraka, the Prophet's second mother.

HALIMA BINT ABI DHUAYB

Halima bint Abi Dhuayb, also known as Halima al-Sa'adia, was a devoted Bedouin wet-nurse to the noble Prophet Muhammad ﷺ. She belonged to the clan of Sa'd bin Bakr, a subsection of the Hawazin, a large north Arabian tribe.

It was the custom in seventh century Arabian society for new mothers of nobility to send their babies to be weaned and raised by Bedouin women. The natural, wild and open desert plains were considered a healthier environment to nurture children in their early years, instead of the closed atmosphere of the city.

Halima travelled to Mecca with her husband, Harith, in the company of women of her clan, seeking babies from among the elite to nurse. Halima reported of that day,

> It was a bad year in our area of the desert. We had nothing to survive on. I was riding a mule and we had with us an old she-camel which

gave us not a drop of milk. We spent many a sleepless night because our little boy was always crying of hunger. I did not have enough milk to satisfy him. Because my mule was also weak, I kept falling behind my companions. I gave them so much trouble because of our weakness.

When they finally reached Mecca, all the Bedouin women found babies to wean, except for Halima. Since Muhammad's ﷺ father was no longer alive, the women knew they could not expect anything in the way of payment, for Amina, although still noble, was now poor.

Halima said,

There wasn't any woman among us who wasn't offered the Messenger of Allah ﷺ, and as soon as a woman was told that he was an orphan she would reject him. We would say, "What is his mother going to give us?" For we only expected recompense from the baby's father. By Allah, each of my friends was able to get a nursling except me. When I did not succeed in getting any [baby] for myself, I told my husband, al-Harith ibn Abdul Uzza, "By Allah, I would not like to be the only one from among my friends who'll go back home without a newborn. I am going to take that orphan boy." My husband said, "You can go and take him. Perhaps, Allah will bless us through him."

Halima's husband could not have spoken a truer word. Halima was overflowing with milk for her new ward as well as her own son, and their camel gave forth an unusual abundance of milk. She said, "As soon as I took him and brought him to my riding animal, I breast-fed him as much as Allah would permit and he drank until he was satiated. His brother also drank until he was satiated. My husband then went to our old camel and milked her and both of us drank until we were satiated. And we passed a good night."

In the morning, Halima's husband told her, "Halima, by Allah, I could see that you have accepted a blessed child. Can't you observe the blessings we have been witnessing since we took him, and Allah continued to increase us in blessing?"

Even their slow, weak donkey which had given so much trouble on the way to Mecca, now had a new energy about it. Halima reported that, "We set out on the journey back to our village. By Allah, my donkey was so fast that none of my friends could catch up with it. Surprised at this, they said, 'Daughter of Abu Dhuayb! Was this not your donkey on which you set out with us?' I said, 'Yes, by Allah, it is!' They then said, 'By Allah, there is something about her!'"

Halima knew that Muhammad ﷺ was no ordinary child. She believed there was a hidden secret in him, unknown except to Allah, which might be revealed one day.

That day did come, but what happened greatly startled Halima. After Muhammad ﷺ had been with Halima for almost four years in the desert, a very strange event occurred. Muhammad ﷺ and his foster brother were playing among the sheep when his brother hurriedly came to his parents, exclaiming, "My Quraysh brother was visited by two men clad in white garments. They laid him on his back and opened his belly!"

Halima and Harith rushed to Muhammad's side, frightened he was dead. But they found him standing and looking pale. His foster father took the young Muhammad ﷺ into his arms and said, "My son, what happened to you?" Muhammad replied, "Two men in white garments came to me. They laid me down and opened my belly. They removed something and took it away. They then returned it as it was."

Later in his life, Prophet Muhammad ﷺ mentioned these incidents of his childhood to his Companions. He told them that two angels came to him in the desert, and one angel made a long incision from the top of his chest down to the base of his abdomen. The angel removed his heart and washed it in a golden bowl "full of faith", and then put Muhammad's heart back in its place. This divine visitation purified the Prophet ﷺ and protected him from being distracted by worldly temptations.

Of course, this was unknown to Halima and her husband, who were deeply disturbed and frightened for their foster son. Harith exclaimed, "Halima, I fear that my son has been touched by (the Jinn). So, let us take him back to his family before any bad consequences emerge."

Halima also felt the safest place for Muhammad ﷺ would be in Mecca with his mother, who was surprised to see them. She exclaimed, "What brought you back, foster parents? You were taking excellent care of him." Halima said, "By Allah, nothing has happened. It is only that Allah has helped us pay our debts and we fear that some harm or unforeseen things might happen to him. That is why we brought him back."

But Amina knew that this could not be the reason and insisted they tell her the truth. Halima told her the entire story. Amina responded,

> So you fear that he might be touched by Satan? No, by Allah! Satan will never be able to find his way to him. By Allah, this boy of mine will have a renowned future. My pregnancy was the easiest any woman has experienced. I saw in my dream that a light came out of me which illuminated all the palaces of Syria. And when I gave birth to him, his delivery was different from that of other babies, he lifted his head to heaven. Leave him with me and go back to your people.

And so it was time for Halima to part from her beloved foster son Muhammad ﷺ. She had loved him dearly and keenly felt the heartache of separation.

Halima managed to visit her foster son over the years, and she saw him grow into a graceful, beautiful young man. She was invited to attend his wedding to the noble Lady Khadija ؓ, who was immensely kind and generous to the woman who nurtured her beloved husband. Halima's flocks had been severely depleted by the widespread drought, so Khadija gifted forty sheep and a camel to Halima, as a mark of honour.

After Muhammad ﷺ attained prophethood, Halima visited him in Medina and he rose to receive her, exclaiming, "My mother, my mother!" Such was the love and affection flowing from his pure heart for Halima bint Abi Dhuayb, the woman who poured milk into his blessed veins.

FATIMA BINT ASAD

After the death of the Prophet's grandfather, Baraka took the orphan Muhammad ﷺ to the house of his uncle, Abu Talib, who was now entrusted with his care. It was in this household that a fourth mother entered the life of Muhammad ﷺ. She was none other than Fatima bint Asad ibn Hashim ibn Abd Manaf, wife to Abu Talib, her cousin.

Fatima bint Asad was the kind natured, noble mother of Ali ibn Abi Talib and his siblings. Muhammad ﷺ was then still only eight years old. Having lost a father he never knew, his beloved mother and his dear grandfather, Muhammad ﷺ was in much need of love, care and comfort.

Fatima bint Asad loved Muhammad ﷺ like he was her own child. She never differentiated between him and her own children. She showered her love on him continuously until he became a young man and was old enough to be independent and get married.

Prophet Muhammad ﷺ was always grateful and loving to Fatima bint Asad. Like a son, he often visited her in her home to ensure she was well and content. When Muhammad ﷺ became a prophet, Fatima bint Asad readily embraced Islam and encouraged her children to do the same. As a widow, she migrated with the Muslims to Medina and died four years later, in 626.

When the Prophet ﷺ heard news of her death, he went to sit beside her body and wrapped his own cloak around her as a burial shroud. He often said, "I was an orphan and she made me her son. No one, after Abu Talib, took better care of me than she did." May Allah have mercy on the fourth mother of Prophet Muhammad ﷺ.

MOTHERS OF THE BELIEVERS

KHADIJA BINT KHUWAYLID

Khadija bint Khuwaylid ﷺ was the best among the women of her time. Noble, intelligent and pious, she was the enduring love of Prophet Muhammad's ﷺ life. Khadija was his first rock of support, the first to believe in his prophecy and the first he looked to for strength and assurance.

Khadija was the daughter of Khuwaylid ibn Asad ibn Abdul Uzza, from the ruling tribe of Quraysh and Banu Asa. She was an incredibly astute, powerful and wealthy businesswoman, who was greatly respected for her excellent character and decency. Her goodness earned her the title "al-Tahira", the pure woman.

She had been widowed twice before she married the Prophet ﷺ. Her first husband was Abu Halah ibn Zarara of the tribe of Banu Tamim, with whom she had two daughters, Halah and Hind. After the death of Abu Halah, she married Ateeq ibn Aiz ibn Abdullah, from the tribe of Banu Makhzum, and after a period of time, they separated.

As a woman of dignity and beauty, she was much sought after in marriage, but she devoted her life to her children and to managing her business affairs. Khadija's servant, Maysara, heard of a man of great moral standing and told his mistress of Muhammad's truthfulness, integrity and impeccable manners. Khadija entrusted Muhammad ﷺ with the management of her trade, and he ﷺ travelled with Maysara to Syria. Prophet Muhammad ﷺ was to prove a great asset to Khadija, and she was highly impressed with his achievements. But what drew her true admiration was Muhammad ﷺ himself.

She was drawn to his noble character, and while she had refused many proposals from the distinguished men of Mecca, she decided she would propose marriage to Muhammad ﷺ herself. But she started to hesitate. Would a twenty-five-year-old man accept the proposal of a forty-year-old woman? Khadija found solace in a wise friend, Nafisa bint Munabbih. Nafisa comforted her and reminded her of Muhammad's ﷺ good character, lineage, wealth and grace, which soared over all those venerable men who sought to marry her.

After speaking with Khadija, Nafisa went directly to Muhammad ﷺ. She intuitively asked him, "Muhammad, why don't you marry?" He answered, "I cannot afford marriage." She smiled and said, "If there is someone who is eligible, would you agree?" He asked, "Who is she?" She said, "Khadija bint Khuwaylid." He said, "I would agree if she did." Nafisa immediately went to Khadija to tell her the good news. Muhammad ﷺ told his uncles Abu Talib and Hamza about his wish to marry Khadija, and they went to Khadija's uncle, Amr ibn Asad, to ask for Khadija's hand in marriage on Muhammad's behalf and settle the dowry.

The day of the marriage arrived, and the celebrations were blessed with happiness and marked with generosity through the distribution of meat among the poor. The wedding party was held in Khadija's house, and among the wedding guests was none other than Halima, who nursed Muhammad ﷺ as a baby. Khadija showed Halima great honour and respect, offering her forty sheep as a gift to the milk mother who suckled her beloved husband Muhammad ﷺ.

Khadija and Muhammad's marriage was a deeply loving and happy union. Such was Khadija's devotion to her husband that when she saw the fatherly affection Muhammad ﷺ had for her slave, Zayd ibn al-Haritha, she gifted Zayd to him. She also lovingly welcomed Ali ibn Abu Talib into her household, who was then only five years old, as Muhammad ﷺ wanted to raise him in their household. Khadija and Muhammad ﷺ were soon blessed with two sons of their own, Qasim and Abdullah. But tragically, they died in infancy. After heartbreak and patience, the couple were eventually blessed with four daughters: Zaynab, Ruqayya, Umm Kulthum and Fatima ﷺ.

Before the birth of all his daughters, Muhammad ﷺ was inclined to worship in solitude. He retreated to a cave on Mount Hira for many days every year, away from the vain talk and materialistic indulgence of the idolatrous people of Mecca. Here, in the cave, he worshipped Allah in tranquil seclusion. Although Khadija could not endure to be away from her beloved Muhammad ﷺ, she knew he needed time away to reflect and have his privacy, so she always had provisions prepared for him.

Many years passed, and the Prophet ﷺ continued to seclude himself in the cave of Hira. Then the day of revelation arrived during the sacred month of Ramadan. The Archangel Jibril ﷺ filled the entire cave and the Prophet's vision with his awesome presence and commanded him to "Read!" The mighty encounter left the Prophet ﷺ in shock. He rushed home pale and trembling, heading straight into Khadija's arms. Frightened and doubting his own sanity, he beckoned his wife, "Cover me, cover me." The cloak that Khadija wrapped him in was mentioned in the Quranic verses, "You, wrapped in your cloak, arise and give warning! Proclaim the greatness of your Lord, cleanse yourself, keep away from all filth, do not be overwhelmed and weaken, be steadfast in your Lord's cause." (74:1–7)

Muhammad ﷺ confided all that had happened and said to his wife, "I am scared, Khadija." This dignified woman replied, "Be steadfast. By Him in whose Hand is Khadija's soul, I pray and hope that you are the prophet of this nation. By Allah, Allah would never humiliate you. You are good to your relatives, you are true to your word, you help those in need, you support those who are weak, you are a good host to your guests and help those in distress."

Khadija's words comforted the Prophet's ﷺ heart. She continued to display wisdom and leadership, knowing that such a momentous time would require even further assurance. She went to her cousin Waraqa ibn Nawfal, a Christian who was learned in the Christian and Jewish scriptures, to tell him what had happened to Muhammad ﷺ. Waraqa proclaimed, "Holy is He, Holy is He! By Him in whose hand is Waraqa's soul, if you are truthful Khadija, it is the great Angel who came to Musa and Isa. Surely, he is the prophet of this nation. Tell him to be steadfast."

Khadija went back to her husband with the good tidings. Then she took her husband to Waraqa so that he ﷺ would internalize the gravity of his mission even further. When Waraqa saw the Prophet ﷺ approaching, he exclaimed, "By Him in whose hand is my soul, you are the prophet of this nation. You will be rejected, hurt, expelled and fought. If I live until such a day, I will support you." Then he gently kissed his head. Muhammad ﷺ asked, "Would they expel me?" Waraqa replied, "Yes. None has claimed what you claim without being fought. I would like to live until such a day."

Waraqa did not live to see that day, but his encouragement was instrumental to the Prophet ﷺ. He ﷺ found an anchor in Waraqa's words and in Khadija's stalwart support. He realised his mission and understood that this was Allah's law concerning His prophets and all callers to Him. Therefore, no matter how severe the suffering or persecution would be, he was ready to meet it.

Khadija was vital to the Prophet's preparation for the call to Islam, and she continued to be a pillar of support during the most severe times of persecution. She brought him relief when he was hurt or rejected. When they called him a liar, she alone remained true.

Khadija was also the first one to learn how to pray from the Messenger of Allah ﷺ. One day, the Prophet ﷺ returned home telling her that Jibril ﷻ had taught him how to pray. She said, "Teach me how he taught you." She then performed ablution alongside the Prophet ﷺ and prayed with her husband, and then said, "Truly, I testify that you are the Messenger of Allah."

Ibn Ishaq said, "Khadija was the first person to believe in Allah and His Messenger and believe in all that he brought. Allah comforted His Messenger by that. The Prophet never heard any unpleasant thing from her whenever she talked to him."

Khadija's life was about to change completely. The Prophet ﷺ told his dear wife that the time of sleep and comfort was over – now was the time for struggle and perseverance. The courageous and resilient Khadija then began to summon people to Islam by her husband's side.

The Muslims suffered many different kinds of chastisement, but Khadija was as steadfast as a mountain. She clung to Allah's statement, "Alif Lam Mim. Do people think they will be left alone after saying 'We believe' without being put to the test?" (Quran 29:1–2)

Khadija faced enormous tests in her life. When Allah took the soul of her two young sons, Qasim and Abdullah, she endured her grief with patience. She also knew how the first martyr in Islam, Sumaya, suffered her fatal trial at the hands of the tyrants. She bid farewell to her daughter, Ruqayya, who emigrated to Abyssinia with her husband, Uthman ibn Affan, to escape the torture of the Quraysh and to preserve her belief. Khadija witnessed times of terrible hardship, but she never became desperate. The more trials she faced, the more patience she exuded.

Khadija was a woman of such distinction that she was given the salutation of peace by the Archangel Jibril himself. The Messenger of Allah told her, "Khadija, here is Jibril. He commanded me to say *salam* to you and to give you glad tidings of a house made of pearls in Paradise, in which there will be no toil or hardship." She replied, "Allah is the Giver of *salam*. Peace be upon Jibril and the peace and mercy of Allah be upon you."

In addition to her own trials, she had to endure seeing her beloved Muhammad suffer hardship. He refused the many attempts that the Quraysh used to entice him away from his belief. In the face of these offers of wealth and power, he swore an oath, "By Allah, my uncle, if they were to put the sun in my right hand and the moon in my left to leave this matter, I would not leave it until Allah discloses His will or until I die."

Thus, Khadija followed Allah's Messenger in belief and perseverance, against all the odds. The Quraysh issued a boycott against the Muslims, the terms of which were written on a scroll that was hung on the Kaaba. They were denied trade, water and food. They were driven out of their homes, and the noble Khadija, lived in the harsh conditions of Abu Talib's valley for three years. She gave all that she had in that trial. She was sixty-five years old by then and the boycott had finally taken its toll. The Prophet was about to face the severest blow — the loss of his beloved, faithful Khadija in a time that was known as the Year of Sorrow. The Prophet was devastated. He had lost his source of comfort, support and abiding love.

Despite the custom to marry many wives, the Messenger of Allah never married anyone else while he was married to Khadija, which was almost two decades. Even after her death, she was never far from Prophet Muhammad's heart. He honoured the special bond between them, sending food to all her relatives and friends. The Prophet never stopped missing Khadija and only spoke of her with the deepest love, nostalgia and reverence.

Later, the Prophet's wife, Aisha, became jealous of the mere memory of Khadija. Aisha said,

> The Messenger of Allah rarely went out of the house without mentioning Khadija and praising her. One day, he spoke of her and I grew

very jealous and I told him, "Was she not an old lady whom Allah has replaced with a better woman for you?" He got angry and said, "No, by Allah! Allah did not replace her with any better woman. For she believed in me when no one else did, she accepted Islam when people rejected me, she comforted me and supported me when people denied me and Allah blessed me with children from her while I was denied children by other women." I said in my mind, "Never shall I speak unfavourably of her again".

Khadija was a truly unique and exceptional woman. Her wisdom, counsel and character were the bedrock of support to the Prophet ﷺ through the most trying years of his prophethood.

The Prophet ﷺ said, "The best of the women of her time was Maryam bint Imran. The best of the women of her time was Khadija bint Khuwaylid." May Allah bless the first Muslim, the first wife and the first love of Prophet Muhammad ﷺ.

SAWDA BINT ZAMA

After the death of his beloved Khadija, no one dared to speak to the Prophet ﷺ about him marrying again. They all knew how much Khadija meant to him, because she alone believed in him when the people rejected him and she alone gave to him when he was poor. No one would come close to his greatest love and support.

After seeing the Prophet ﷺ so alone, Khawla bint Hakeem, one of the Prophet's earliest companions, was the only woman brave enough to broach the topic of marriage. She said to the Prophet ﷺ, "Will you not marry, Messenger of Allah?" He answered sadly, "Who could replace Khadija?" She said, "Whoever you like. There is a virgin and a widow." He said, "Who is the virgin?" She cleverly answered, "the daughter of the one you love most, Aisha bint Abu Bakr." Then the Prophet ﷺ asked, "Who is the widow? She replied, "Sawda bint Zama."

Sawda bint Zama ibn Abdul Qays of the Banu Amir of Quraysh ﷺ was a noble and venerable lady. Her mother was Shamus bint Qays ibn Zayd ibn Amr of Banu Najjar. She was first married to al-Sakran ibn Amr, who accepted Islam in the first year of Muhammad's ﷺ prophethood. She and her husband emigrated to Abyssinia along with eight others of Banu Amir, leaving their homes far behind them to escape the torture of the Quraysh. On their return from Abyssinia, her husband died and Sawda was left a widow. Her cousin and brother-in-law, Suhayl ibn Ami al-Amiriy, said he would take her in if she gave up Islam. But Sawda refused. She was committed to her faith. She lived with her ageing father and was herself around fifty years old.

The Prophet ﷺ had great sympathy and esteem for this widow. Sawda had migrated twice for the sake of Islam, once to Abyssinia and then to Medina. As soon as Khawla bint Hakim mentioned her to him, he wanted to stand by Sawda, especially because she was older, alone and needed someone to care for her. All the people of Mecca wondered how the Prophet ﷺ could marry such an old widow who had lost all her beauty. How could she take the place of the mistress of Quraysh? While no woman could ever take the place of Khadija, the Prophet ﷺ showed Sawda compassion and consideration and decided to marry her.

Khawla went to tell Sawda the good news, saying, "Would you like Allah to give you great blessing, Sawda?" Sawda asked, "And what is that, Khawla?" She said, "The Messenger of Allah has sent me to you with a proposal of marriage!" Sawda tried to contain herself in spite of her utter astonishment and then replied in a trembling voice, "I would like that! Go to my father and tell him that." Khawla went to Zam'a, an old man, greeted him and then said, "Muhammad son of Abdullah son of Abdul Muttalib has sent me to ask for Sawda in marriage." The old man exclaimed, "A noble match! What does she say?" Khawla replied, "She would like that." He told her to call Sawda to him. When she came, he said, "Sawda, this woman claims that Muhammad son of Abdullah son of Abdul Muttalib has sent her to ask for you in marriage. It is a noble match. Do you want me to marry you to him?" Sawda said she accepted, feeling the great honour bestowed upon her.

The Prophet ﷺ married Sawda ﷺ, who remained his only wife for about three years. She began to manage the Prophet's household and take care of his daughters, Umm Kulthum and Fatima, alongside her own six children, according to some sources. Sawda was known to be tall, slow and overweight, yet she had a clean heart and was deeply committed to her faith. She was amiable and humorous, dispelling the Prophet's worries and sorrows with the warmth of her wit.

One day she saw the Prophet ﷺ look pale and distressed. She wanted to lighten his heart and make him smile and so told him jokingly, "O

Messenger of Allah. I prayed behind you yesterday and you prolonged the prostration so long that I felt like I was having a nose-bleed." The Prophet ﷺ laughed so much that his molars were visible, and his gloom lifted. As well as making him smile, Sawda also stood by her husband with firm loyalty and faith. When the Meccans mocked the Prophet ﷺ after his description of the Night Journey to Jerusalem and from there to the heavens, it was Sawda who believed in him ﷺ.

When Aisha, Hafsa, Zaynab, Umm Salama and others came to the Prophet's house as wives, Sawda realised that the Prophet ﷺ had only married her out of sympathy after her husband's death. The Prophet ﷺ worried that she might be upset that his other wives were much younger than her. When she heard that the Prophet ﷺ wanted to kindly separate from her to release her from such a position, she felt as though it was the worst thing that could happen. She entreated the Prophet ﷺ saying, "O Messenger of Allah, hold me. By Allah, I did not seek to have a husband, but I just hope that Allah may resurrect me as your wife on the Day of Judgement." She preferred the Prophet's desires over her own, and she granted her night to Aisha to please the Prophet's heart. The Prophet ﷺ was moved by her action. Then Allah revealed, "If a wife fears high-handedness or alienation from her husband, neither of them will be blamed if they come to a peaceful settlement, for peace is best. Although human souls are prone to selfishness, if you do good and are mindful of God, He is well aware of all that you do." (Quran 4:128)

Sawda was very close to Aisha, and Aisha remembered her fondly, saying, "I never saw a woman who was more beloved to me to emulate than Sawda bint Zama who, when she grew old, said, 'O Messenger of Allah I have granted my day to Aisha.' " (Muslim)

Sawda remained in the Prophet's house, brimming with gratitude to Allah for inspiring a solution that allowed her to retain her position as a mother of the faithful and to be a wife of the Prophet ﷺ in Paradise. She lived until the days of Umar's caliphate and died having lived a long life of piety, goodness and generosity. May Allah be pleased with Sawda, a mother of the believers.

AISHA BINT ABU BAKR
Aisha bint Abu Bakr was one of the most extraordinary, intelligent and astute women that ever lived. She is considered one of Islam's greatest

scholars. She was born to noble parents of high moral calibre and excellent character. Her father, Abu Bakr Abdullah ibn Abu Quhafa of the Quraysh, was the closest friend of Prophet Muhammad ﷺ. Aisha's mother, Umm Romaan, had previously been married to Harith ibn Abdillah al-Azdi who entered into alliance with Abu Bakr but died soon afterwards. Abu Bakr married the widow as a sign of honour for the alliance and as a mark of respect for the friendship between him and her former husband. Umm Romaan had two children with Abu Bakr, Abdul Rahman and Aisha. Abu Bakr had two other children, Abdullah and Asma from his other wife.

Aisha's mother was a courteous, generous and beautiful woman. The Prophet ﷺ visited the house of his greatest friend every day, and Umm Romaan always received the Prophet ﷺ with great hospitality. When Khawla bint Hakim brought news to Umm Romaan of the Prophet's proposal to Aisha, she was overjoyed, knowing that it would bring great blessings.

Abu Bakr had brought fine red striped cloth from Bahrain to make into a wedding dress, and Aisha's long hair was combed and decked in ornaments. The wedding ceremony was very simple; there was no wedding feast but the newlyweds drank from the same bowl of milk. The couple did not live together until three years later (some accounts say five), after the Battle of Badr.

The age of Aisha when she entered the Prophet's household as a wife has been a point of contention and difference of opinion, based upon differing dates. Scholars have placed her age ranging from nine years old to nineteen years old.

Some arguments include, according to the eighth century Ibn Sa'd in '*al-Tabaqat*', that Aisha was engaged to a man named Jubair ibn Mut'im before she married the Prophet ﷺ, which means she would have already been reaching maturity. Also, Fatima, the Prophet's daughter, was five years older than Aisha, which means Aisha would have been around ten when she was married and thirteen or fifteen when she lived with him as his wife (as some stated that the marriage was consummated five years after the ceremony).

Imam Wali al-Din Muhammad ibn Abdullah al-Khatib in his famous Hadith collection, '*Mishkat al-Masabih*', commented that Asma, Aisha's sister, was ten years older than her and died in 73 AH at the age of 100.

This would make Aisha eighteen in 1 AH, so Aisha would have been nineteen at the consummation of her marriage. Ibn Kathir also stated the same about Aisha and Asma's ages.

In the earliest detailed biography of the Prophet ﷺ, Ibn Ishaq lists fifty-one people who accepted Islam in the early days of the Message, before it was in its fifth year. The list does not include children. Ali, who was only ten or twelve when he embraced Islam, was not included in the list, yet Aisha was. If her age is maintained to be six at the time of her wedding, she would have allegedly been only a one-year-old baby when she embraced Islam.

Returning to the account of Aisha, around two years after the Hijra, the bride then moved into the new house of the Prophet ﷺ, which consisted of a room beside the mosque built of clay and palm trees. The room was furnished with a mattress of palm leaves, beneath which there was nothing but a mat. In such a modest room, Aisha began her blessed marriage to the Prophet Muhammad ﷺ.

Aisha was to become the most beloved person to the Prophet ﷺ. Amr ibn al-As related that he asked the Prophet ﷺ, "Who do you love most, O Messenger of Allah?" He replied, "Aisha." The Messenger of Allah told Aisha, "You have been shown to me in (my) dreams on three nights. An angel was carrying you in a silken cloth and said to me, 'This is your wife.' And when I uncovered it, behold, it was you. I then said, 'If this dream is from Allah, He will cause it to come true.'"

The Prophet ﷺ often called her by the nickname Humaira, meaning "reddish skin" in Arabic, as she had a rosy pigmentation. He also affectionately and playfully called her a shorter version of her name, 'Aish'. As for the Companions, they gave her the title al-Siddiqa, meaning "the one who affirms the truth". Aisha was a true daughter of her father Abu Bakr, al-Siddiq.

The relationship between the Prophet ﷺ and Aisha was profoundly loving, romantic and intimate. There are many accounts narrated by Aisha that provide wonderful insights into their marriage and convey how they shared everything together, even how they bathed together. Whenever they ate together, Aisha would take a sip of water and pass it to the Prophet ﷺ who would sip from the same spot her lips touched. She related, "[The Prophet] would call for a drink and insist that I take it first before he drank from it. So I would take it and drink from it, then put it down, then he would take it and drink from it, putting his mouth where mine had been on the cup" (Sunan al-Nasai).

Another instance of tenderness is when Aisha placed her chin on the shoulder of the Prophet ﷺ while watching some children play. He asked her if she was done watching and she kept saying no so she could stay resting on his shoulder (Jami al-Tirmidhi). There was also playfulness; Aisha fondly recalled memories of racing with the Prophet ﷺ and winning the race when she was younger and fitter, but when she was older and plumper, she would observe how she could no longer outrun him ﷺ.

Once, a delegation arrived in Medina from Abyssinia and they displayed their spear skills in front of the Prophet ﷺ. Aisha stood behind the Messenger of Allah ﷺ, resting her head upon his noble shoulder so that she could watch them and amuse herself. She stayed in this position until the Prophet ﷺ asked if she had seen enough, and she said that she had.

Once, the other wives of the Prophet ﷺ highlighted a grievance about receiving gifts which displeased him and led to him defending Aisha and demonstrating his special regard for her. Aisha relates,

> The people used to send presents to the Prophet on the day of my turn. My companions [i.e. the other wives of the Prophet] gathered in the house of Umm Salama and said, "O Umm Salama! By Allah, the people choose to send presents on the day of Aisha's turn and we too love the good [i.e. presents] as Aisha does. You should tell Allah's Messenger to tell the people to send presents to him wherever he may be, or wherever his turn may be." Umm Salama said this to the Prophet and he turned away from her and when the Prophet turned back to her, she repeated the same, and the Prophet turned away again, and when she told him the same for the third time, the Prophet said, "O Umm Salama! Don't trouble me by harming Aisha, for by Allah, the Divine Inspiration never came to me while I was under the blanket of any woman amongst you except her" (Bukhari).

Yet Aisha ﷺ loved the Prophet ﷺ so much, that she was prone to being jealous and never more so than of the memory of Khadija. Aisha said,

I am not jealous of the other wives of the Prophet as I am jealous of Khadija. This is due to the Prophet's constant mentioning of her and as Allah had commanded him to give her glad tidings of a house in Paradise of precious stones. And when he sacrificed a sheep he would send a fair portion of it to her friends. Occasionally, I would say to him, "It is as if there had never been any other woman in the world except Khadija!"

One day, the wives of the Prophet ﷺ, including Aisha, complained to each other that the poor, ascetic life they had to live was becoming too trying for them. They agreed to ask that he give them more of the little luxuries in this world, but the Prophet ﷺ could never let his wives enjoy more while the people suffered. He refused their demands and did not visit his wives for an entire month until these verses were revealed, "Prophet, say to your wives, 'If your desire is for the present life and all its finery, then come, I will make provision for you and release you with kindness. But if you desire God, His Messenger and the Final Home, then remember that God has prepared great rewards for those of you who do good' " (Quran 33:28-30). Then the Prophet ﷺ asked Aisha to consult her parents and decide whether she wished to remain with him. Aisha replied, "Should I consult them concerning you? Never. I certainly choose Allah and His Messenger."

Aisha readily chose to endure poverty and hunger with her beloved ﷺ. It is related that they spent two or three months without cooking and would only eat dates and water. When the Muslims became wealthy, she was once given 100,000 dirhams as a gift. But as she was a woman of great generosity, by the evening she had distributed it among the poor until there was not a single dirham left. She was also fasting that day and had barely enough bread to break her fast on. Her maid asked her, "Why didn't you reserve a dirham in order to buy meat for your meal?" Aisha answered, "Do not worry about that now. Had you reminded me, I would have." Another time that Aisha was fasting, she had one piece of bread for her iftar, when a poor man begged for some food. She told her maid to give him the bread, but the maid said, "If I give him the piece of bread, you will have nothing for your iftar." Aisha replied, "I don't mind, let him have it."

The most critical incident in Aisha's life was the incident of the *ifk* (lie). On the return from the expedition of Banu Mustalaq, something occurred that would injure both Aisha and the Prophet's honour. When the march was ordered, Aisha was not in her tent, having gone to search for a valuable necklace she had dropped. As her palanquin was veiled and she herself was so light in weight, it was not noticed that she was not seated in it until the army reached the next halt. Meanwhile, finding the camp had moved on without her, she sat down to rest, hoping that someone would come back to fetch her when her absence was noticed. It was night, and she fell asleep. The next morning, she was found by Safwan, a Muhajir. He had been left behind to pick up anything inadvertently left behind. He put her on his camel and brought her to the caravan, leading the camel on foot. This presented an occasion for the Prophet's enemies to raise a malicious slander. The ringleader among them was the chief of the hypocrites in Medina – Abdullah ibn Ubay.

Aisha stayed at her parents' home during this testing time and was in extreme anguish for an entire month because of the slander that was being spread about her. Aisha's mother, Umm Romaan, tried to assure her daughter, but Aisha said, "Glory be to Allah! I have spent the entire night until morning unable to stop weeping and could not sleep at all. Morning found me still weeping." The Prophet ﷺ tried to defend Aisha's honour by calling the community to the mosque, but the hypocrites were ready to make matters even worse.

The Prophet ﷺ went to see Aisha, telling her that if she were innocent, Allah would protect her honour, but if she had made a mistake, then she should seek forgiveness and Allah would pardon her. Then Aisha's tears stopped falling, she displayed true strength of character and replied, "By Allah, I can only say what the father of Yusuf said – patience is beautiful and Allah is my protection against what you describe." Allah the Most High Himself defended Aisha from dishonour, sending down these verses and silencing the slander,

> It was a group from among you that concocted the lie. Do not consider it a bad thing for you [people], it was a good thing and every one of them will be charged with the sin he has earned. He who took the greatest part in it will have a painful punishment. When you heard the lie, why did believing men and women not think well of their own people and declare, "This is obviously a lie"? And why did

the accusers not bring four witnesses to it? If they cannot produce such witnesses, they are the liars in God's eyes. If it were not for God's bounty and mercy towards you in this world and the next, you would already have been afflicted by terrible suffering for indulging in such talk. When you took it up with your tongues and spoke with your mouths things you did not know [to be true], you thought it was trivial but to God it was very serious. When you heard the lie, why did you not say, "We should not repeat this. God forbid! It is a monstrous slander"? God warns you never to do anything like this again, if you are true believers. God makes His messages clear to you. God is all knowing, all wise. (Quran 24:11-18)

During the Prophet's illness, after returning from the farewell pilgrimage, he felt that death was near. It is narrated that when the Prophet ﷺ was being carried to each of his wives' houses to spend his nights, he would ask, "Where do I go tomorrow? Where do I go tomorrow?" He was hoping it would be Aisha's turn. The mothers of the believers, out of compassion and respect, offered their turns to Aisha so that the Prophet ﷺ could receive care from whom he most wanted it. They said, "O Messenger of Allah, we give our turns to Aisha."

The Prophet ﷺ then moved to Aisha's home, where she tended to him day and night. She would say, "I would sacrifice my father and mother for you, O Messenger of Allah." At the last moment of the Prophet's life, in his final breath, his head lay in Aisha's lap.

She said,

The Prophet ﷺ died on the night of his usual turn at my house. Allah took him unto Him while his head was between my chest and my neck and his saliva was mixed with my saliva, for Abdul Rahman ibn Abu Bakr entered holding a soft *siwak*. The Prophet ﷺ looked at the *siwak*. I thought that he wished to brush his teeth with it. I took the *siwak*, chewed and then perfumed it. Then I gave it to the Prophet ﷺ, who in turn brushed his teeth very well. As he returned it back, his hand fell down. I began to supplicate to Allah with a *dua* often said by Jibril ﷺ and also by the Prophet ﷺ during his illness. However, the Prophet ﷺ did not supplicate Allah with this *dua* at this time. He looked skyward and said, "The Highest Companion," to the heavens. Then he died. Praise be to Allah who mixed my saliva with his at the last moment of the Prophet's life.

The Prophet ﷺ was buried where he died, in Aisha's home.

Aisha was a woman of generosity, piety and incredible character, yet above all she was an exceptional scholar. She constantly learned from the Prophet ﷺ and was one of three wives who memorised the entire Quran. Aisha was a *muhadditha*, a narrator of hadiths. She is one of four companions who transmitted over 2,000 sayings, having narrated more than 2,210 hadiths, of which 174 are commonly agreed upon by Bukhari and Muslim.

It is claimed by Islamic scholars that without Aisha half of the knowledge and understanding of the Sunnah would have disappeared. Aisha ﷺ showed the world how women excelled in scholarship, medicine, poetry, politics and warfare. Both men and women came from afar to learn from her wisdom, and it was said that the number of female students outweighed their male counterparts. As well as providing answers to their questions, she also took in girls and boys, some of them orphans, to train them in their education. Her home thus became a centre of learning and her students were outstanding. Among them was her own nephew, Urwah, who became a distinguished reporter of hadiths. Among the women was Umrah bint Abdul Rahman who became a trustworthy narrator of hadiths and acted as Aisha's secretary, handling the letters addressed to Aisha. Aisha promoted education among women and men and remains an eminent source of authorization and documentation in Hadith transmission and sacred law.

Some of Aisha's accolades from other Companions and compilers of Islamic history include the following:

Abu Musa al-Ash'ari said, "Whenever a hadith was unclear to us, we asked Aisha about it and we always gained knowledge about that hadith from her."

Masruq ibn al-Ajda said, "I saw the elders among the Companions of Muhammad asking her about the law of inheritance.'

Al-Zuhri said, "If Aisha's knowledge is compiled and compared to the knowledge of all women, her knowledge will surely excel theirs." He also said, "The first person to remove distress from the people and explain to them the Sunnah regarding that, was Aisha."

Aisha was a brilliant orator, the military general al-Ahnaf ibn Qays said, "I have heard speeches of Abu Bakr and Umar, Uthman and Ali and the *khulafa* up to this day, but I have not heard speech more persuasive and more beautiful from the mouth of any person than from the mouth of Aisha."

Aisha's nephew, Hisham ibn Urwa said, "I have never seen anyone who had better knowledge of a Quranic verse, an obligatory action, a supplemental action, poetry, history, lineage, judgement or medicine better than Aisha. I asked her, 'What about medicine? How did you learn it, Aunt?' She answered, 'When I was sick, the Prophet would prescribe a treatment for me as he did when the people were ill. I also heard the people prescribing treatment to each other. I memorised such prescriptions.'"

Once, Masruq was asked, "Did Aisha perfect the obligatory acts?" He answered, "By Allah, I have seen the great prophetic Companions asking her about the obligatory actions."

The tenth century born Persian scholar, Hakim al-Nishapuri, said in his five-volume Hadith collection, *'al-Mustadrak'*, "One fourth of the rule of *sharia* was narrated on the authority of Aishah."

Aisha lived for nearly fifty years after the Prophet's death and was his wife for a decade. Her knowledge, intelligence and esteemed scholarship played a crucial role in the prophetic legacy. After the death of Muhammad ﷺ, Aisha was regarded as the most reliable source in the teachings of Hadith. She died in 58 AH, having lived to see the rules of four caliphs. May Allah be pleased with Aisha bint Abu Bakr, the scholarly mother of the believers.

HAFSA BINT UMAR

Hafsa was a deeply pious and beautiful woman who became the Guardian of the Sacred Quran. She was the daughter of the great Umar ibn al-Khattab, and like her father, she was of a strong, stern character. She married Khunis ibn Hudhafa ibn Qays al-Sahami, a Qurayshi man who went on the two emigrations to Abyssinia and then to Medina. He fought in the battles of Badr and Uhud, the latter in which he was fatally wounded and died shortly thereafter, leaving Hafsa a young widow.

Umar was so deeply saddened for his widowed daughter, who was eighteen years old, that whenever he saw his daughter grieving, he grieved as well. After a long period of reflection, he decided to choose a husband who would bring light back into her heart.

He first thought of Abu Bakr ◉, the dearest person to the Prophet ◉. Umar went at once to Abu Bakr to offer him Hafsa's hand in marriage, thinking he would not refuse to marry his own daughter, who was herself such a pious, noble young woman. But Abu Bakr sympathetically listened to him, yet did not respond.

Umar returned home brokenhearted and could not believe what had happened. He then went to Uthman ibn Affan, whose wife Ruqayya had recently died. Umar repeated what he said to Abu Bakr, but Uthman apologised saying, "I think I would not like to marry at the present time." Umar's gloom increased with both Uthman's and Abu Bakr's refusal and he became angry at his two closest friends. He went to the Prophet ◉ complaining about Abu Bakr and Uthman. The Prophet ◉ smiled and said, "Hafsa will marry someone better than Uthman, and Uthman will marry someone better than Hafsa" (Bukhari).

The Prophet ◉ meant he himself would marry Hafsa. He wanted to give equal honour to both Abu Bakr and Umar and nothing would show them greater honour than marrying their daughters as a reward for their truthful sincerity and their sacrifices for the sake of Islam. Umar was elated to receive a prestige greater than he had imagined and was so happy that he shared his news with everyone he met. When Abu Bakr met him, he realized the source of his joy. He congratulated him and apologized, "Do not be angry with me, Umar. The Prophet had mentioned Hafsa before, and I could not disclose the Prophet's secret ◉. Had he not thought of her for himself, I would have married her."

The marriage between Hafsa bint Umar and the Prophet ◉ took place in the month of Shaaban in the third year of the Hijra, and all of Medina rejoiced. Uthman married Umm Kulthum bint Muhammad ◉ in the month of Jumad al-Thani in the same year. Thus, it was that the Prophet ◉ was married to the daughters of his closest friends, Aisha, daughter of Abu Bakr, and Hafsa, daughter of Umar.

Now both wives of the Prophet ◉, Hafsa and Aisha, became very close, almost as if they were sisters. Yet there were times that Hafsa and Aisha backed each other up against the Prophet ◉. Consequently, Allah the Almighty said, "If both of you [wives] repent to God – for your hearts have deviated – [all will be well]. If you collaborate against him, [be warned that] God will aid him, as will Jibril and all righteous believers, and the angels too will back him. (Quran 66:4)

Hafsa was totally devoted to her faith. She would fast often and stay awake to perform the night prayers to come ever closer to her Lord. She resembled her father in devotion as well as character, for Hafsa's nature was somewhat stern, tough and argumentative. When she lost her first husband, this sternness became even more pronounced and she was easily irritated. One day, Hafsa's mother was having a disagreement with Umar and he said, "Are you arguing with me, woman?" and she replied, "Why not? Your daughter keeps arguing with the Messenger of Allah to the point of upsetting him for the whole day." On hearing this, Umar went directly to his daughter's house to chastise her, but the Prophet ﷺ would not let him go anywhere near her.

Some sources narrate that the Prophet ﷺ divorced Hafsa. But he took her back according to Jibril's command, "Take Hafsa back. She constantly fasts and prays in the night and will be your wife in Paradise."

Uqbah ibn Amir's narration of this incident relates that when Umar heard that the Prophet ﷺ was going to divorce Hafsa, he poured sand over his head and said, "Allah will no more care about Umar and his daughter after she has been divorced [by the Prophet]." So Angel Jibril came to the Messenger of Allah the following day and told him, "Allah commands you to take her back as a way of showing compassion to Umar."

Hafsa realized the gravity her behavior, and after the Prophet ﷺ forgave her, she was keen never to annoy the Prophet ﷺ again. She lived in harmony with the Prophet ﷺ in Medina for eight years until he died, and she lived on for another thirty-four years, witnessing the expansion of the Muslim empire under her father's leadership and then under Uthman's caliphate.

Hafsa had a rare skill at that time. She was able to read and write, and she had committed the entire Quran to memory. After the Prophet ﷺ died and Abu Bakr ؓ succeeded him, it was Hafsa who was chosen to safeguard the first copy of the Quran. It had been written by Zayd bin Thabit on Abu Bakr's instructions and was given to Umar for safekeeping, and Umar then entrusted it to Hafsa. Under Uthman's caliphate, it was this copy of the Quran, in Hafsa's keeping, that was

I had just about reached Tanim [about three miles from Mecca] when I met Uthman ibn Talha [He was a keeper of the Kaaba in pre-Islamic times and was not yet a Muslim]. "Where are you going, Bint Zad al-Rakib?" he asked. "I am going to my husband in Medina," I responded. "And there isn't anyone with you?" he asked. "No, by Allah. Except Allah and my little boy here," I replied. "By Allah, I shall never abandon you until you reach Medina," he vowed. He then took the reins of my camel and led us on. I have, by Allah, never met an Arab more generous and noble than he. When we reached a resting place, he would make my camel kneel down, wait until I dismounted, lead the camel to a tree and tether it. He would then go to the shade of another tree. When we had rested, he would get the camel ready and lead us on. He did this every day until we reached Medina. When we got to a village near Quba [about two miles from Medina] belonging to Banu 'Amr ibn 'Awf, he said, "Your husband is in this village. Enter it with the blessings of God." Then he went back to Mecca.

After a long and difficult separation, Umm Salama was finally reunited with her husband. They were overjoyed to see each other again and to begin a new life together in Medina. Umm Salama had been the first woman to emigrate to Medina, just as she was the first woman to journey to Abyssinia, and at long last, she found a home.

In Medina, she devoted her life to rearing her children. Abu Salama fought bravely in the battles of Badr and Uhud and was injured by an arrow in his forelimb. He treated the wound until he thought that it was healed, but it had not and would later claim his life.

Two months after Uhud, the Prophet ﷺ was informed that Banu Asad were gathering to attack him in Medina. He held Abu Salama in high esteem and appointed him as the leader of about 150 men, including Abu Ubaydah and Saad ibn Abu Waqqas, to attack them in the mountain of Qutn. Following the Prophet's instructions, Abu Salama attacked the enemy in the morning before they were prepared, and the Muslims were victorious. In addition to the spoils of war, they also restored the Muslims' position, which had been affected in Uhud.

In this battle, Abu Salama's wound that he suffered in Uhud reopened. He could not leave his bed for treatment, and he said to his wife, "Umm Salama, I heard the Messenger of Allah ﷺ say that when a Muslim meets a catastrophe and says, 'To Allah we shall return' and then says, 'O Allah! May You reward me for my catastrophe and replace it with something better,' then they will get what they ask for."

Ziyad ibn Maryam narrated that Umm Salama told Abu Salama, "I heard that if the husband of a woman dies and he is one of the inhabitants of Paradise and his wife did not remarry after him, Allah will join them together in Paradise. The same thing applies to men." Abu Salama then told his wife, "I am making a pledge with you that I will not marry after and you will not marry after me." He then asked her, "Will you obey me?" Umm Salama said, "If I did not want to obey you I would not have consulted you." Abu Salama said, "If I die you should remarry." He then said, "O Allah! Provide for Umm Salama after me a man who is better than me and who will not disgrace her or harm her." Umm Salama said, "When he died I said, 'Who is that man that will better than Abu Salama?'"

One day the Prophet ﷺ went to visit Abu Salama but found that he was on his death bed, for soon after he arrived, Abu Salama died. The Prophet ﷺ closed Abu Salama's eyes with his honourable hands, then he looked skyward and said, "O Allah! May you forgive Abu Salama, raise his ranks among the closest people, succeed him in his family and forgive us and him, O Lord of Worlds."

Umm Salama bore the loss with a faithful heart and a patient soul. She surrendered to Allah's destiny and remembered what Abu Salama narrated on the authority of the Prophet ﷺ. She began to supplicate, "O Allah reward me for my catastrophe . . ." but she was reluctant to complete the second part of the *dua*, ". . . and replace it with something better". She could not imagine who would be better than her late husband. However, she completed the *dua* as an act of devotion to Allah.

After her waiting period had ended, many great Companions proposed marriage to her. It was the custom of the Muslims at that time to safeguard widows by marrying them, but Umm Salama rejected every proposal. The Prophet ﷺ reflected on the honourable, clever, faithful and patient Umm Salama. A woman who had emigrated twice in Allah's cause, a woman who had suffered anguish and heartbreak yet remained strong in her faith. He thought that he could not possibly leave Umm Salama to go through life without a husband by her side.

One day, she was tanning the hide of an animal when one of the used to make several copies to send to the corners of the rapidly expanding Muslim empire.

Hafsa never ceased in her devotion to Allah until her death ﷻ in 47 AH at the age of sixty-three. May Allah grant mercy to Hafsa bint Umar, the guardian of the Quran.

ZAYNAB BINT KHUZAYMA

Zaynab bint Khuzayma was a noble woman of deep piety and great generosity. She gave so much to the poor and needy that she earned the title, "Mother of the Poor". Zaynab was the half-sister of Umm al-Fadl and Maymuna, one of the Prophet's later wives. The three sisters had the same mother but different fathers.

Zaynab embraced Islam in the early days of the Prophet's mission. She then married Abdullah ibn Jahsh and migrated with him to Abyssinia to escape the terrible persecution the Muslims were facing in Mecca. Abdullah was the Prophet's ﷺ cousin, as his mother was Umamah bint Abdul Muttalib. Zaynab and Abdullah were utterly dedicated to Islam. Their piety was exemplary, and they were both people of extraordinary humility.

The Messenger of Allah ﷺ appointed Zaynab's husband as the first leader of a group of Muslims on an expedition; he was the first to be called "Amiral-Mu'minin" (Commander of the Believers). The Prophet ﷺ admired Abdullah's sincerity and resilience and told his Companions, "I will certainly send a man who is most enduring of hunger and thirst among you."

It was in the third year after the Hijrah that Abdullah was martyred in the Battle of Uhud. He was not only killed, but was mutilated on the battlefield. But this was what he himself had prayed for. Before the battle, he said to his friend Sa'ad ibn Abi Waqqas, "O Allah! Let me meet a sternly furious man whom I will fight in Your cause and let him take hold of me and cut my nose and ears so that when I meet You I will say, 'This is in Your cause and in the cause of Your Messenger' and You will say, 'You have said the truth.'" Sa'd said, "The supplication of Abdullah was better than mine. I saw him later on that day with his nose and ears hanging in a thread."

Al-Zubayr ibn Bakkar narrated, "Abdullah ibn Jahsh used to be called 'the one who was mutilated in Allah's cause.' His sword was broken in the Battle of Uhud and the Messenger of Allah ﷺ gave him a thin dry rod which turned into a sword while in his hand. Thereafter he was nicknamed 'the thin dry rod'. "

Zaynab was in a well of grief, and the Messenger of Allah ﷺ came to know of her pain and loneliness on losing her beloved husband. The Prophet ﷺ was moved by her sorrow and wished to support and look after the grieving widow and so proposed marriage to her. Zaynab's heart filled with relief and joy at the honour of being the Prophet's wife, and she accepted without hesitation.

They married in 4 AH, when Zaynab was thirty years old. Zaynab had a beautiful and kind nature, and lived in harmony with the Prophet's wives, Aisha, Sawda and Hafsa. Her generosity to the poor never stopped flowing. Once a poor man came to her house to beg for some flour. She gave him the last of her own, and she herself went without food that night. Muhammad ﷺ had so much admiration for her compassion that he told the other wives about her goodness, and said, "If you have faith in Allah, He would provide for your sustenance, even as He does for the birds, who leave their nest hungry in the morning, but return full at night."

Zaynab's marriage to the Prophet ﷺ was brief. Only eight months (some accounts say less than two years) into the marriage, Zaynab became seriously ill. This illness turned out to be fatal, and she died four years after Hijra.

She was the only wife of the Prophet ﷺ who died during his lifetime, other than Khadija. The Prophet ﷺ carried her body into the grave and was deeply saddened by her death. He invoked Allah to forgive her and he always remembered her for her patience and perseverance. May Allah have mercy on Zaynab bint Khuzayma, the generous mother of the faithful.

UMM SALAMA

Umm Salama, or Hind bint Umayyah ibn al-Mughira al-Makhzumiyya, was gifted with wisdom, grace and beauty and was to become an outstanding scholar. She was a member of the elite tribe of the Quraysh and her father was a prominent leader known by his nickname "Zad al-Rakib", meaning "provision of the traveller". He earned this title because he would provide for anyone who accompanied him while travelling, no matter how long the journey. Zad al-Rakib was famous for being one of the most generous men of the preIslamic era in the Arabian Peninsula. As for Umm Salama's mother, she was Atika bint Amir ibn Rabia al-Kananiyya, aunt to the Prophet Muhammad ﷺ and from Banu Firas.

Besides her honourable and well-established lineage, Umm Salama was an intuitive woman. She married Abdullah ibn Abdul Asad al-Makhzumi (the Prophet's cousin and foster brother) and together they were among the earliest followers of Islam in Mecca. She stood by her husband and suffered many kinds of torture with him in the way of Allah. But it came time for them to escape the endless persecution. Umm Salama became the first woman to emigrate to Abyssinia, leaving the familiarity of her home to travel to a new land where, together, she and her husband could practise their faith in peace. It was in this place of refuge that Umm Salama gave birth to their first child, Salama.

After the charter of the boycott against the Muslims had been nullified and Hamza and Umar had embraced Islam, which greatly strengthened their cause, the emigrants were finally able to return to Mecca. Umm Salama and Abdullah were grateful to be back in their homeland, but the persecution did not stop.

After the conclusion of the Pledge of Aqaba between the Messenger of Allah and the Ansar of Medina (the Aws and Khazraj tribes), the Prophet ﷺ gave the Muslims permission to emigrate to Medina. Umm Salama and Abu Salama decided to uproot once more. But Umm Salama was about to face another test, even more traumatic than she had faced before. A test in which her family would be torn apart in front of her very eyes. We hear it in her own words,

> When Abu Salama [my husband] decided to leave for Medina, he prepared a camel for me, hoisted me on it and placed our son Salama on my lap. My husband then took the lead and went on without stopping or waiting for anything. Before we were out of Mecca however, some men from my clan stopped us and said to my husband,
>
> "Though you are free to do what you like with yourself, you have no power over your wife. She is our daughter. Do you expect us to allow you to take her away from us?" They then pounced on him and snatched me away from him. My husband's clan, Banu Abdul Asad,

saw them taking both me and my child. They became hot with rage, "No! By Allah," they shouted, "we shall not abandon the boy. He is our son and we have a first claim over him." They took him by the hand and pulled him away from me. Suddenly in the space of a few moments, I found myself alone and lonely. My husband headed for Medina by himself and his clan had snatched my son away from me. My own clan, Banu Makhzum, overpowered me and forced me to stay with them. From the day my husband and my son were separated from me, I went out at noon every day to that valley and sat at the spot where this tragedy occurred. I would recall those terrible moments and weep until night fell on me."

Umm Salama stated that she continued to visit that spot for an entire year, weeping for the loss of her son and husband and feeling anguish at their forced separation. But her fate was about to change. She recounts,

> I continued like this for a year or so until one day a man from the Banu Umayyah passed by and saw my condition. He went back to my clan and said, "Why don't you free this poor woman? You have caused her husband and her son to be taken away from her." He went on trying to soften their hearts and play on their emotions. At last they said to me, "Go and join your husband if you wish." But how could I join my husband in Medina and leave my son, a piece of my own flesh and blood, in Mecca among the Banu Abdul Asad? How could I be free from anguish and my eyes be free from tears were I to reach the place of the Hijrah not knowing anything of my little son left behind in Mecca? Some realised what I was going through and their hearts went out to me. They petitioned the Banu Abdul Asad on my behalf and moved them to return my son. I did not even want to linger in Mecca till I found someone to travel with me, and I was afraid that something might happen that would delay or prevent me from reaching my husband. So I promptly got my camel ready, placed my son on my lap and left in the direction of Medina.

Umm Salama left Mecca alone with her child Salama clutched to her. But then, three miles outside of Mecca, she was blessed with another guardian. She relates,

Prophet's Companions asked for permission to enter. She offered him a pillow to sit upon. He then conveyed that the Prophet ﷺ himself proposed marriage to her. Umm Salama was amazed and could barely believe what she had heard. But she recalled the hadith related by Abu Salama, ". . . and replace my catastrophe with something better" and realised that this was certainly the best replacement.

Yet out of her honesty, humility and openness, she did not hesitate to disclose her flaws to the Prophet ﷺ. She sent a message back saying, "O Messenger of Allah, who would not wish to marry you? But I have three characteristics. I am a woman who is extremely jealous and I am afraid that you will see in me something that will anger you and cause Allah to punish me. I am a woman who is already advanced in age and I am a woman who has a young family." The noble Prophet ﷺ sent this reply, "Regarding the jealousy you mentioned, I pray to Allah the Almighty to let it go away from you. Regarding the question of age you have mentioned, I am afflicted with the same problem as you. Regarding the dependent family you have mentioned, your family is my family."

Umm Salama graciously accepted the Prophet's ﷺ proposal and she said, "Allah substitutes Abu Salama for the one who is better than him, the Messenger of Allah ﷺ." Thus, Umm Salama became a mother of the believers, taking a position of honour in the Prophet's household. Her sound judgement and astute intelligence gained the love and respect of the Prophet's other wives, and she would often be the mediator between them.

Significantly, Umm Salama was a source of wisdom for the Prophet ﷺ who heeded her advice in relation to the Treaty of Hudaybiya. This treaty was named after a stopping place around nine miles outside of Mecca. The Prophet ﷺ had been approaching the city with 1,400 Muslims to perform Umrah but the Meccans refused them entry into the city.

Muhammad ﷺ agreed to abandon the pilgrimage on the condition they could return the following year. The treaty between Muhammad ﷺ, representing the state of Medina, and the Quraysh tribe of Mecca in 628 / 6 AH was a pivotal one. It aimed to begin a ten-year truce to diffuse the tensions and grant political and religious recognition to the growing community of Muslims in Medina.

Yet many Companions felt frustrated with the terms of the treaty, as it appeared to make too many concessions to the Quraysh. Before the treaty took place, everybody had bought sacrificial animals with them in the hopes of completing the rites of Umrah. The Prophet ﷺ ended his *ihram* and commanded his Companions to slaughter their animals, but the Companions refused. The Prophet ﷺ repeated his command three times to no avail. Finally, he went home and related what had happened to Umm Salama. She ؓ listened carefully and advised, "O Messenger of Allah, if you want the Muslims to do what you want, you should go out and not speak with anyone until you slaughter your own camel and have your own hair cut." The Prophet ﷺ agreed and followed her counsel. As soon as the people saw the Prophet ﷺ doing that, they started to slaughter their animals and cut their hair. And so, through her wise judgement and insight, Umm Salama prevented dissent and division among the Muslims.

Umm Salama was indeed an extraordinary woman. She was involved in many significant battles, aiding soldiers and tending to the wounded. Away from the battlefield, she had the gift of being able to speak and write beautiful poetry and prose.

Like Aisha and Hafsa, Umm Salama memorised the Quran, and several verses were revealed in her own home. Allah gave her great honour by permitting her to see Jibril ؑ in human form. Umm Salama was very knowledgeable about religious matters and narrated no less than 387 hadiths and issued many *fatwas*. Abdullah ibn Abbas, one of the most learned Companions of the Prophet ﷺ who committed to memory around 1,660 sayings of the Prophet ﷺ which are recorded and authenticated in the collections of al-Bukhari and Muslim, used to consult with Umm Salama on Islamic law.

Following the death of Prophet Muhammad ﷺ, Umm Salama's scholarship became even more important and many people, including men and women from all walks of life, used to seek her counsel. She had many students and placed great emphasis on teaching women even though she taught men as well. Her daughter, Zaynab, is said to be her greatest student and became a prominent scholar.

Umm Salama lived a long life and witnessed many crucial events, trials and battles, yet remained neutral throughout. According to many reports, she always called to harmony and mutual love among the Muslims.

Umm Salama had been married to the Prophet ﷺ for seven years and lived for many more decades after his death until she was the last to die of the Prophet's wives. She passed away in the month of Dhul Qaadah in 61 AH at the age of eighty-four. Abu Huraira read the funeral prayer over her. Allah grant Umm Salama, the scholarly wife, mercy and Paradise.

UMM HABIBA RAMLA BINT ABU SUFYAN

Ramla was one of the prominent women of her time and was gifted with wisdom, gentleness and generosity. She was the daughter of Abu Sufyan, the leader of the Quraysh, who was a bitter enemy of the Prophet ﷺ and did not embrace Islam until much later. Yet Ramla bravely entered into Islam, despite her father's opposition.

She married Ubaydulla ibn Jahsh and together they embraced Islam in the House of Arqam, where the Muslims secretly met in the early days of the Message. Despite Abu Sufyan's attempts, he could not convince the steadfast Ramla to forsake Islam and remain a pagan. Here was the powerful leader of the Qurash, powerless to prevent his own daughter from following Muhammad ﷺ. But the other members of the Quraysh took their vengeance against Ramla and her husband, making their lives unbearable.

The couple decided to retreat to Abyssinia and find refuge with the compassionate Christian ruler, The Negus. Leaving her homeland far behind her in Mecca, Ramla travelled the rugged roads, exposed to the heat and dangers of the desert and armed only with scant provisions. She undertook all this while she was expecting her first child. A few months after reaching their destination in Abyssinia, she gave birth to a daughter, Habiba, and was henceforth known as Umm Habiba.

Umm Habiba showed just how resilient and patient she was, having suffered alienation and oppression from her own family and tribe. Now, as a refugee in Abyssinia, she was about to be tested again.

One night, she had a bad dream in which she saw her husband in the midst of a fathomless ocean covered by wave upon wave of darkness. She said, "My husband, Ubaydulla ibn Jahsh, appeared disfigured. In the morning, I found out that he had converted to Christianity. I told him what I had seen in my dream but he did not care about that."

Ubaydulla had lost his Muslim identity and did his best to convert his wife. But she held fast to her belief and begged him to remain a Muslim, yet he refused. He began to drink wine excessively and was often drunk, and after some time, he died of his addiction. Umm Habiba was distressed at the state of his passing. She was now a widow in a land far from home. Years passed, yet she endured every challenge that came her way. She devoted her days to worship and to raising her daughter. She kept Allah's promise close to her heart, "...Anyone who believes in God and the Last Day should heed this. God will find a way out for those who are mindful of Him and will provide for them from an unexpected source. God will be enough for those who put their trust in Him. God achieves His purpose. God has set a due measure for everything" (Quran 65:2–3).

Umm Habiba had another vivid dream, yet this time it held hope and promise. She dreamt that someone called out to her saying, "Mother of the Faithful". When she woke up, she felt sheer joy. By now, the Prophet ﷺ had established the first Islamic state in Medina and he was brought news of Abyssinia. He learned of Umm Habiba's situation and sent a message with Amr bin Umayyah to The Negus, the king of Abyssinia, who was now a Muslim. The message held an offer of marriage to Habiba, if she willed it.

The Negus promptly sent his slave girl, Abraha, to Umm Habiba with the message from the Prophet ﷺ. When Umm Habiba received the news, she was so overwhelmed with happiness that she removed all her silver jewellery – her anklets, bangles and rings – and gave them to Abraha saying, "May Allah bless you!" She then sent word to her relative, Khalid bin Said ibn al-As, requesting that he conduct the marriage. The Negus was commissioned by the Prophet ﷺ and that very evening, he gathered all the Muslims in Abyssinia, headed by Jafar ibn Abu Talib, the Prophet's cousin.

The Negus delivered a speech to the wedding guests saying,

> Praise be to Allah, the Sovereign, the Holy One, the Source of Peace [and Perfection], the Guardian of Faith, the Preserver of Safety, the Exalted in Might, the Irresistible, the Justly Proud. I testify that there is no god but Allah and Muhammad is the Messenger of Allah about whom Jesus son of Mary foretold. To proceed, the Messenger of Allah sent me a message and asked me to give him Umm Habiba bint Abu Sufyan in marriage. Therefore, I do what the Messenger of Allah asked. I give her four hundred dinars as a dowry.

Then he poured out the dinars before the people. Afterwards, Khalid ibn Said spoke,

> Praise be to Allah. I praise Him and seek His help. I testify that there is no god but Allah and Muhammad is His servant and His Messenger, whom He sent with the guidance and the religion of truth and that He will make it prevail over all religions, even though the pagans may detest it. To proceed, I responded to what the Messenger of Allah asked. Thereby, I give him Umm Habiba bint Abu Sufyan in marriage. May Allah bless their marriage.

Then The Negus held the wedding feast, welcoming the guests to enjoy its blessings and saying, "It is the sunnah when marrying to offer food." Umm Habiba, who was brimming with happiness, sent for Abraha again. She apologized for not rewarding the slave girl properly earlier and gifted fifty dinars to make herself clothes and jewellery. Abraha had a gift for Umm Habiba too. She presented her with a small bag of expensive perfumes, which were wedding presents from The Negus' wives. Abraha had embraced Islam but kept her new faith a secret. She was happy to receive Umm Habiba's generosity but wished for one thing most of all – to send a message to the Prophet ﷺ via his new bride. All she asked was if Umm Habiba would convey her greetings to the Prophet ﷺ in person, as this would be the greatest favour she could do for a poor woman such as herself.

Umm Habiba set out for Medina with the returning emigrants and told the Prophet ﷺ all about the generosity of The Negus, what life was like in Abyssinia and of course she did not fail to convey Abraha's greetings to him. The Prophet ﷺ was very pleased with her message and returned her greetings and prayed that Allah would bless Abraha abundantly.

The Prophet ﷺ and Umm Habiba consummated their marriage in the sixth or seventh year after the Hijra to Medina. Meanwhile, the Quraysh had breached the truce of Hudaybiyah. Fearing that matters would get even worse, Umm Habiba's father, Abu Sufyan headed out to Medina as an envoy of the Quraysh to apologise to the Messenger of Allah ﷺ and reaffirm the truce. The first thing Abu Sufyan did when he arrived at Medina was to go and see his daughter, whom he had not seen for many years. Umm Habiba coldly received him. She loved her faith so much that she valued it above all ties of kinship. Only Allah and His Messenger ﷺ were important to her now.

When Abu Sufyan wanted to sit down upon the Prophet's mat, Umm Habiba folded it and put it away. He said, "O daughter, I do not know whether it is better for me to sit upon this mat or not." She quietly answered, "It is the Prophet's mat and you are a disbeliever and impure. Therefore, I do not like you to sit upon it." He said, "O daughter, you have surely been seized by something evil after you left me." She firmly answered, "It is better to say, 'Allah guided me to Islam.' O father, you are the leader of Quraysh. I wonder how you could miss out on entering Islam. You only worship deaf and blind stones." Abu Sufyan asked her how he could possibly turn his back on a religion his forefathers had followed for generations. He left his daughter's house in frustration.

But Umm Habiba yearned for her father and her brother, Muawiyah, to enter into the fold of Islam. After years of their refusal to embrace the faith, Umm Habiba's constant wish and prayers came true. At the peaceful conquest of Mecca by the Muslims, Abu Sufyan and Muawiyah, who was to become the fifth Caliph of Islam, pledged allegiance to the Prophet ﷺ. Umm Habiba could not contain her joy. The following verses were revealed,

"God shall bring about affection between you and your present enemies. God is all powerful, God is most forgiving and merciful" (Quran 60:7).

Once, Muawiya visited the Prophet ﷺ and found Umm Habiba seated beside him. When he turned to leave, the Prophet ﷺ called out and invited him to join them. The Prophet ﷺ said that he sincerely wished that all three of them would sit like this again enjoying the pure drink of Paradise, suggesting they would be reunited in the Garden.

If Umm Habiba attained the promise of Paradise for one aspect of her life alone, it would be for her immense knowledge. Due to her wisdom, eloquence and mastery in Hadith, she was ranked fourth among the Mothers of the Believers. First was Aisha bint Abu Bakr, the second was Umm Salama and the third was Maymuna bint al-Harith. Umm Habiba narrated sixty-five hadiths, including one that referred to the mourning period of a widow, of four months and ten days. Another hadith related to *miswak*, when Umm Habiba relates that the Prophet ﷺ said, "If it had not been so difficult, I would have liked my *ummah* to clean their teeth with *siwak* before every prayer just as they perform ablution with every prayer." Another relating to the voluntary prayers at noon stated, "Whoever observes the practice of offering four *rakahs* before Duhr prayer and four *rakahs* after it, Allah will shield him against the fire of hell."

When she was on her death bed, Aisha relates, "Umm Habiba called me when she was about to die and said, 'There might have been between me and you what usually happens between rivals. Will you please forgive me?' So I forgave her and asked Allah to forgive her. She then said, 'You have made me happy, may Allah make you also happy.' And she went to Umm Salama and asked her the same."

Umm Habiba passed away in Medina in 44 AH during the caliphate of Muawiya. She was seventy years old. May Allah bless Umm Habiba, a master in Hadith.

ZAYNAB BINT JAHSH

Zaynab bint Jahsh bint Rabab ibn Yamur, known as Barra before the Prophet ﷺ married her, was the daughter of Umayma, the Prophet's aunt from his paternal side. Zaynab was a devoted worshipper, incredibly generous and submitted to Allah's will even if it was against her own wishes.

This was shown nowhere more clearly than in her marriage to Zayd ibn al-Haritha. Zaynab came from the highest branch of the Bani Asad clan and was deeply proud of her noble lineage. She was also a beautiful woman and had been offered many proposals of marriage from young Qurayshi men, but she rejected them all.

Then the Prophet ﷺ betrothed her to Zayd, a former slave. Zayd had a special place in the Prophet's heart ever since he was a young boy. Zayd had been gifted to Muhammad ﷺ by Khadija ﷺ and the Prophet ﷺ later freed and adopted him. Zaynab and her family were dissatisfied with the proposed union to someone who had been a slave. Zaynab looked down on Zayd and, in addition to her objection to his status, Zayd was not physically attractive. But the Prophet ﷺ had his reasons for the marriage and said, "I like it for you." Zaynab protested, "O Messenger of Allah, I do not like it for myself. Moreover, I am the most beloved single woman in my family and I am your cousin. Thus, I could not do that." Then Allah the Almighty revealed the following verses, "When God and His Messenger have decided on a matter that concerns them, it is not fitting for any believing man or woman to claim freedom of choice in that matter. Whoever disobeys God and His Messenger is far astray" (Quran 33:36).

Zaynab offered no further protestations but faithfully, albeit reluctantly, submitted to the command of Allah and the Prophet ﷺ and married Zayd. The marriage was deeply symbolic; it held up the Islamic principle that all people are equal and that none can be preferred to another except in piety.

However, it turned out to be an unhappy union. Even though both Zaynab and Zayd were excellent people in their own way and both loved the Prophet ﷺ, there was a mutual incompatibility that proved detrimental to married life. Zaynab would often remind Zayd of her nobility and Zayd could no longer bear the condescension. He went to the Prophet ﷺ and told him he wanted to divorce his wife. But the Prophet ﷺ asked him to hold off and to fear Allah, even though he ﷺ already knew there would be a divorce and that he himself would be commanded by Allah to marry her.

The Prophet wanted to prove a vital point that would contradict the pagan taboo about adopted sons and marrying their divorced or widowed wives. But the Prophet ﷺ did not tell Zayd or anyone else what the higher purpose of the marriage had been. He feared that people, and especially the disbelievers, would circulate that Muhammad ﷺ had married his son's wife. Then Allah revealed these verses,

> When you [Prophet] said to the man who had been favoured by God and by you, "Keep your wife and be mindful of God," you hid in your heart what God would later reveal. You were afraid of people, but it is more fitting that you fear God. When Zayd no longer wanted her, We gave her to you in marriage so that there might be no fault in believers marrying the wives of their adopted sons after they no longer wanted them. God's command must be carried out. (Quran 33:37)

Al-Waqidi stated that this verse was revealed while the Prophet ﷺ was talking to Aisha at home. He began to shiver and when he had recovered, he smiled and said, "Who would go to give glad news to Zaynab?" Then he recited the verse. Ibn 'Abbas reported that, "When Zaynab heard the news of her divorce from Zayd and her engagement to the Prophet she prostrated to Allah (in gratitude)."

So a year after Zaynab and Zayd's wedding, they divorced, and then Zaynab ؎ married the Prophet ؎ without a *wali* (guardian) or witnesses. The contract of marriage was stated in the verses of the Quran itself, and Zaynab was incredibly honoured by the distinction afforded to her. She once said to the Prophet ؎, "O Messenger of Allah! I am not like your other wives. There is none among them whose father, brother, or family had not married her off to you except me. But Allah conducted my marriage from above His throne." In another version, she said, "Allah conducted my marriage in heaven." And in another version she said, "Allah conducted my marriage from above the seven heavens."

Zaynab was a righteous, pious and devoted Muslim. She spent many days in fasting and many nights in prayer. Zaynab ؎ was skillful in leatherwork, would tan hides and weave clothes, giving everything she made to the poor and needy.

Aisha said of her, "I have never seen a woman who is better than Zaynab in religion, piety, truthfulness, keeping good terms with kin, charity and doing devotional work." Aisha also said, "Once, the Prophet ؎ said to his wives, 'The one who will die first after me is the one with the longest hand.'" Aisha narrated that the Prophet's wives would go to a wall and stretch up their hands in order to know which of them has the longest hand. Aisha states, "After the Prophet's death, we gathered together and compared our hands. We kept doing that until Zaynab bint Jahsh died. She was not bigger than us, and it was then that we realized that the Prophet ؎ had meant the longest hand which gives charity."

When Aisha was wrongfully accused of adultery and most people turned against her, it was Zaynab who defended her. When the Prophet ؎ asked Zaynab's opinion on Aisha during a time fraught with tension, Zaynab said she did not want to defile her ears listening to the slander. She swore by Allah that she found Aisha to be a truly God-fearing woman of exemplary character and that she found the traits of sincerity, honesty and integrity in Aisha. She emphasised how she saw nothing but goodness and virtue in her. Aisha later narrated that she never forgot how Zaynab stood by her at the worst time of her life, when the world was against her.

The Prophet ﷺ was very fond of her and would often seek her company. She once received some special honey from a relative and it happened to be the Prophet's favourite. Whenever she offered him the honey, he enjoyed savouring the taste of it and spent even more time with her than the other wives. Yet Aisha, Hafsa and Sawda, out of sheer love and yearning for the Prophet ﷺ to come to them sooner for their turn in his blessed company, devised a plan. They decided they would each tell him that there was a peculiar smell emanating from his mouth, hoping he would think they meant the honey. The Prophet ﷺ was very particular about personal hygiene and he stopped eating the honey and decided he would never eat it again. Then Allah revealed these verses: "Prophet, why do you prohibit what God has made lawful to you in your desire to please your wives? Yet God is forgiving and merciful" (Quran 66:1).

Zaynab was the first of the Prophet's wives to die after him. On her death, Aisha said, "A grateful and devout person and a haven for orphans and widows has passed away." The leader of the believers, Umar ibn al-Khattab, prayed over her body and the people of Medina walked in her funeral procession. Zaynab bint Jahsh died in 20 AH at the age of fifty-three, may Allah be pleased with this generous mother of the believers.

SAFIYA BINT HUYAY

Safiya bint Huyay ibn Akhtab ibn Sayah was descended from the blessed bloodline of prophets. She traced her lineage to Prophet Harun who was from the tribe of al-Lawi ibn Israel ibn Ishaq ibn Ibrahim ﷺ. Safiya was chaste, rational, wise, beautiful, religious and came from a noble family. Before Islam came to Arabia, she was married to Sallam ibn Abu al-Huqaiq. She then married Kinana ibn Abu al-Huqaiq. Both of her husbands were Jewish poets.

Safiya's father, Huyay ibn Akhtab, was one of the most dangerous and treacherous leaders in Medina. He was leader of the Banu Nadir, one of the biggest Medinan Jewish tribes. The Prophet ﷺ made treaties and pacts with these tribes, but they broke the terms of the treaties and went back on their binding oath. The Prophet ﷺ went to the leaders to resolve an issue of compensation. While the Prophet ﷺ and his Companions were welcomed outwardly, Huyay ibn Akhtab secretly suggested they should seize the opportunity to kill the Prophet ﷺ. Angel Jibril ؑ warned the Prophet ﷺ, who stood up quietly and left.

As punishment for their treachery, the Prophet ﷺ ordered Banu Nadir to leave Medina. They refused and instead fortified their forts. A battle ensued and the Banu Nadir were overcome. The survivors left the city and went to Khaybar where they conspired against the Prophet ﷺ.

Huyay then allied himself with polytheists and the Jewish tribe of Banu Quraydha to fight against the Muslims. He was killed in the battle. The Muslims then conquered Khaybar and Safiya's husband, Kinana, was killed and Safiya was captured along with all the other Jewish women.

Bilal, the Prophet's muezzin, led Safiya and her cousin through the place of conflict where the bodies of many Jewish men lay. Safiya kept strong and patient and did not cry, but her cousin could not contain her grief. She slapped her cheeks, wept and wailed and poured earth on her head. They were brought before the Prophet ﷺ and ordered that the wailing woman be taken away from his presence. He said, "Did mercy forsake you, Bilal, that you led two women through the death place of their men?"

Subsequently, the Prophet ﷺ and Safiya decided to marry after her waiting period had expired. The Prophet ﷺ afforded Safiya's freedom as a dowry on the condition she would accept Islam. She agreed, and after a period of time in Khaybar, he left with Safiya placed on the mount of a camel just behind him. The wedding banquet consisted of the food of Khaybar, which was a simple feast of dates, milk and butter.

The Prophet ﷺ noticed a greenish tinge around Safiya's eyes and asked her the reason for it. She said, "When I got married to Kinana, I saw a dream in which the sun descended upon my chest. When I awoke, I told my dream to Kinana. He got angry and slapped my face. He said, 'Would you like the King of Hijaz, Muhammad?'" The trace of this blow was still on her face. Anas ؓ narrates,

> The Prophet ﷺ stayed for three days at a place between Khaybar and Medina. There he consummated his marriage with Safiya bint Huyay. I invited the Muslims to a banquet, which included neither meat nor bread. The Prophet ﷺ ordered leather dining sheets to be spread and then the dates, dried yogurt and butter were placed on it, and that was

the banquet of the Prophet ﷺ. (Bukhari)

When they reached Medina, the Prophet ﷺ decided it would be better for Safiya if she did not stay in apartments along with his other wives. Instead, he preferred that she stay in the house of his Companion, Haritha ibn al-Numan.

When the women in Medina knew she was coming, they looked forward to seeing her beauty for themselves. Ibn Sa'd narrated on the authority of Ata ibn Yasar that he said, "When Safiya arrived from Khaybar, she lodged at a house belonging to Haritha ibn al-Numan. The women heard of that and they came looking at her beauty and Aisha also came wearing her face veil. When she came out, the Messenger of Allah asked her, 'What did you see?' She said, 'I saw a Jewish woman!' He then told her, 'Do not say that. For, she has embraced Islam and practices it perfectly.' "

When Safiya moved to the Prophet's house, the other wives of the Prophet ﷺ were jealous of her beauty. They would boast that they were Arabs, while she was a foreigner. These comments upset the Prophet ﷺ, who defended Safiya whenever she was treated without respect. Ibn Sa'd narrated on the authority of Aisha,

> The Messenger of Allah was on a journey and a camel became ill and Zaynab bint Jahsh had an extra camel. So he said to her, "Safiya's camel is ill, can you please give her a camel?" But Zaynab said, "Should I give (a camel) to that Jewish woman?" So the Messenger of Allah ﷺ deserted her for Dhul-Hijjah and Muharram, two or three months without coming to her, Zaynab said, "Until I gave up all hope in him."

Once, Safiya was informed that Hafsa said that she was the daughter of a Jew and she began to weep. When the Prophet ﷺ found her weeping, he asked, "Why do you weep?" She replied, "Hafsa said that I am the daughter of a Jew." Then the Prophet ﷺ said, "You are the daughter of a prophet, the niece of a prophet and the wife of a prophet. Thus, how could she boast over you?" Then he said to Hafsa, "Fear Allah, Hafsa." Safiya loved the Prophet ﷺ deeply and cherished his wise words. Whenever anyone said anything to her, she often replied, "Why, I am Muhammad's wife, Harun's daughter and Musa's niece."

Safiya was a woman of great forbearance and intelligence. It is related that during the caliphate of Umar, she had a servant who went to him and said, "Safiya loves Saturday and has connections with the Jews." Umar sent for Safiya to investigate the case. She replied, "As for Saturday, I have not loved it since Allah gave me Friday in its place, and as for the Jews, I have kinfolk among them and maintain my family ties." When Safiya asked her servant what made her do that, she said, "the devil". Safiya responded, "You may go now, you are free."

The Prophet ﷺ declared Safiya's quality of truthfulness in front of his wives when he was sick, an illness that would later claim his life. Ibn Sa'd reported on the authority of Zayd ibn Aslam who said,

> The Prophet's wives gathered [around him] when the Messenger of Allah ﷺ was in his sickness, [the same sickness] due to which he passed away. Safiyyah [may Allah be pleased with her] said, "O Prophet of Allah! I wish I was suffering from that which you are suffering from!" Upon hearing this, the Prophet's wives began winking at each other. The Messenger of Allah ﷺ commanded them, "Go and rinse your mouths." They said, "From what?" He said, "Because of your winking at one another in order to mock her. By Allah! She is truthful [in what she said]."

Even after the Prophet's death, Safiya lived among the believers as one of the mothers of the believers, and was honoured and abundantly respected. She had memorized many hadiths of the Prophet ﷺ and the people in turn narrated them from her.

Safiya bint Huyay died in Medina in 52 AH during the caliphate of Muawiya. She was buried beside the other mothers of the believers ﷺ. May Allah grant her peace.

JUWAYRIYA BINT AL-HARITH

Juwayriya bint al-Harith, formerly named Barra, was renowned for her great piety, spiritual discipline and beauty. She was the daughter of Harith ibn Abu Dirar ibn Labib al-Khuzaiyya, the chief of Banu Mustalaq, and was married to her cousin, Mani ibn Safwan, one of their most influential leaders. Banu Mustalaq was one of the tribes that waged war against Islam – they clung to their pagan beliefs and wished to destroy the Prophet ﷺ and end his influence. They gathered weapons to prepare an attack on Medina.

The Prophet ﷺ was gifted with extraordinary leadership qualities and had appointed highly qualified men among his Companions to monitor the movement of the enemy. The sinister intentions of Banu Mustalaq thus became known through the Prophet's intelligence sources. As an experienced commander, Prophet Muhammad ﷺ decided to launch a sudden attack to quell the uprising of Banu Mustalaq near a well called alMuraysia.

The battle of Muraysia left Juwayriya a widow and she was taken as a prisoner of war. When the spoils were distributed among the warriors, Juwayriya was in the share of Thabit ibn Qays ibn al-Shammas. She was around twenty years old.

She first tried to escape slavery by offering Thabit ibn Qays money in exchange for her freedom. She then went to the Prophet ﷺ asking for help. She began her address, "O Messenger of Allah! I am Juwayriyah, the daughter of al-Harith, the leader of his people. You are not oblivious to what has happened to me. I fell in the share of Thabit ibn Qays and agreed with him to ransom myself, so help me to free myself." The Prophet ﷺ sympathised with her and said, "Would you like something better than that?" She anxiously said, "What is it, Messenger of Allah?" He said, "I will pay on your behalf and then marry you." She said, "Yes, O Messenger of Allah."

Juwayriya addressed the Prophet ﷺ as the Messenger of Allah as she had already embraced Islam, despite being the daughter of the Prophet's enemy. Diffusing the prior animosity, it was Juwayriya's union with the Prophet ﷺ that brought abundant blessings to her people, as Aisha ﷺ narrates,

> When the people found out that the Prophet ﷺ had married Juwayriyya bint al-Harith ibn Abu Dirar, they started saying, "Will the Prophet's in-laws be held as captives?" Then the people freed all the captives that were with them of the tribe of Banu Mustalaq, and the number of those freed reached 100 households because of the Prophet's marriage to Juwayriyah. I have never known a woman who was a greater blessing for her tribe.

Aisha, the mother of the believers, added, "She was very beautiful and captivated whoever saw her. When she came to the Prophet ﷺ to negotiate her freedom, by Allah, no sooner did I see her standing by my door than I grew jealous. I expected that the Prophet ﷺ would realize what I realized."

And so the pious, beautiful bride of Banu Mustalaq joined the Prophet's household, and this is when the Prophet ﷺ changed her name from Barra to Juwayriya. Changing the names of his Companions was a known habit of the Prophet ﷺ, whether male or female. He did this so that his Companions would shun anything which was related to the time of ignorance. There are different opinions as to why he ﷺ changed the name of a number of his female Companions from 'Barra' to another name. One opinion stated that 'Barra' is derived from the word 'birr', which means righteousness. The Messenger of Allah ﷺ disliked that a people should praise themselves with such a name.

One time, Juwayriya's father, al-Harith, set out for Medina to complain to the Prophet ﷺ about his daughter's capture. He had brought 100 camels with him in exchange for her release but when he came close to Medina, he noticed how two camels stood out in better quality from the rest. He decided to put them aside so that they would not be among the camels for ransom. He tied them up in a secret place and assigned some guards to watch over them.

He then entered the mosque and greeted the Prophet ﷺ who welcomed his wife's father warmly. Al-Harith requested that the Prophet ﷺ give his daughter back to him and the Messenger of Allah ﷺ asked, "Would you like to give her the choice?" Her father agreed, saying his daughter could return with him if she liked, but she said, "I have chosen Allah and His Messenger." Al-Harith asked the Prophet ﷺ to accept the ransom, and the Prophet ﷺ in turn asked with a smile, "What about the two camels you set aside and tied up in such and such place?" Al-Harith was speechless and visibly amazed. He then spoke the following words, "I testify that there is no deity worthy of worship except Allah and that you, Muhammad, are a Messenger of Allah! By Allah! No one knows of this matter except Allah alone."

Al-Harith returned to his tribe a Muslim and informed them about what happened, which led to all members of the Banu Mustalaq tribe embracing Islam. This was a manifestation of Allah's blessing upon Juwayriya and her tribe, through His Messenger ﷺ.

Juwayriya herself was entirely devoted to Islam and spent many hours in worship, often from dawn to the noon prayer. Ibn Abbas narrates from Juwariya,

> The Prophet prayed Fajr prayer and then left her apartment. He stayed out until forenoon and then came while she was still at her place of prayer. She told him, "I have remained here ever since you left." The Prophet ﷺ thereupon told her, "I have recited four words three times after I left you and if these are to be weighed against what you have recited since morning, these would outweigh them and [these words] are, 'Praise be to Allah according to the number of His creation and according to the pleasure of His Self and according to the weight of His Throne and according to the ink [used in recording] words [for His Praise] [Subhanallahi wabihamdihi 'adada khalqihi wa ridha nafsihi wa zinata 'arshihi wa midhadha wa kalimatihi].' "

We also learn through Juwariya the conditions around fasting on a Friday and coupling it with a fast the day before or following. It was narrated, "The Messenger of Allah visited her on a Friday while she was fasting. He asked her, 'Did you fast yesterday?' She said, 'No.' He said, 'Are you going to fast tomorrow?' She said, 'No.' Thereupon he said, 'Then, break your fast.' "

Juwariyah had memorized many valuable hadiths and was a treasure chest of noble traditions and lessons. She lived until the fiftieth year after the Hijra, having reached the age of sixty-five. When she died, the then governor of Medina, Marwan ibn al-Hakam, led her funeral prayer. May Allah grant Juwayriya mercy, a woman whose marriage with the Prophet ﷺ was a source of great blessing for herself and her tribe and for Muslims throughout the centuries.

MAYMUNA

Maymuna bint al-Harith ibn Hazan ibn Bujayr was among the women of Quraysh who were famous for their honour and nobility. She came from an illustrious family of intellectuals, warriors and martyrs.

Among her sisters was Umm al-Fadl, who had the great honour of being the second woman, after Khadija, to accept Islam. Umm al-Fadl was married to al-Abbas, son of Abdul Muttalib, the Prophet's grandfather. There was also Lubaba Sughra, whose son, Khalid bin Walid, earned the title "Saifullah", meaning "The Sword of Allah", as he broke nine swords in the intensity of battle against the Romans. Maymuna's other sister, Salma bint Umays, was the wife of Hamza, the Prophet's uncle who was known as the "Lion of Allah".

Maymuna was thus of the Ahlul Bayt (the people of the House). She was extremely pious, righteous and gentle. Aisha's described her as "among the most pious of us and the kindest to kith and kin."

Maymuna's first marriage was to Masud ibn Amr al-Thaqafi before Islam came to the Arabian Peninsula. After the Prophet ﷺ began receiving the Message, Maymuna frequently visited her sister, Umm al-Fadl. Her heart was moved by hearing stories of the Muslims and learning of their beautiful faith. Maymuna was in her sister's house when she heard news that the Muslims had returned victorious from the battle of Khaybar, and she found herself feeling joyous about their victory. But when she returned home, she found her husband disappointed and depressed. They quarrelled and separated from each other, and she went to al-Abbas' house.

When the Prophet ﷺ and the Muslims came to stay in Mecca for three days to perform their rites, as stated in the Treaty of Hudaybiya, they entered Mecca peacefully on the appointed day. They loudly chanted, "*Labbayk Allahumma labbayk, labbayka la sharika laka labbayk* [Ever at Your service, O Allah, ever at Your service. Ever at Your service, You have no partner, ever at Your service]."

All of Mecca was affected by the clamour; their victorious return shook the land beneath their enemies' feet. They retreated to the mountains on the outskirts of the city so as not to witness Muhammad ﷺ and the Muslims returning to Mecca so strong. However, some remained – they were the men and women who secretly professed the faith of Islam. They had been waiting for the day of victory to come so that they might finally declare their faith publicly. Maymuna was among them. She also told her sister, Umm al-Fadl, of her wish to join the Prophet's house as his wife. In turn, her sister told her husband, al-Abbas and commissioned him to take a proposal to the Prophet ﷺ. The Prophet ﷺ accepted the proposal and gave her four hundred dirhams as dowry. In another version, it is stated that it was Maymuna who proposed marriage herself to the Prophet ﷺ. Allah the Almighty revealed,

Prophet, we have made lawful for you the wives whose bride gift you have paid, and any slaves God has assigned to you through war and the daughters of your uncles and aunts on your father's and mother's sides, who migrated with you. Also, any believing woman who has offered herself to the Prophet and whom the Prophet wishes to wed – this is only for you [Prophet] and not the rest of the believers. We know exactly what We have made obligatory for them concerning their wives and slave-girls, so you should not be blamed. God is most forgiving, most merciful. (Quran 33:50)

After the Prophet ﷺ stayed in Mecca for three days as per the Treaty of Hudaybiya, the people of Quraysh asked him to leave. The Prophet ﷺ kindly asked, "Would you let me wed amongst you, and I would invite you to the wedding feast?" But they harshly replied, "We do not need your food; we just want you to leave." What the polytheists feared most was the Prophet's presence amongst them because they knew the powerful impact he had on people's hearts.

The Prophet ﷺ gave the Muslims permission to leave, while his marriage was incomplete. On reaching Sarif, a place ten miles away from Mecca, Maymuna and the Prophet ﷺ consummated the marriage in the month of Shawwal, in the seventh year of the Hijra. She was said to be around thirty-six years old at the time of her wedding and was the last of the Prophet's wives.

After their marriage, the following verse was revealed, "You [Prophet] are not permitted to take any further wives, nor to exchange the wives you have for others, even if these attract you with their beauty. But this does not apply to your slave-girls. God is watchful over all" (Quran 33:52).

The Prophet ﷺ gave his last wife the new name of Maymuna, which means "blessed" as she had until then been called Barra. Maymuna was true to her new name and provided a window to some blessed narrations. She used to pray in the Prophet's mosque and heard him say that one prayer in the Prophet's mosque is equal to a thousand prayers in all other mosques, except Masjid al-Haram.

Maymuna is also associated with the '*dua* of light'. It was related by Ibn Abbas, who was Maymuna's nephew, that he once stayed as a guest with Maymuna and the Prophet ﷺ. When the Prophet ﷺ awoke for night prayers, Ibn Abbas joined him and among the supplications of the Prophet ﷺ was what became known as the *dua* of light. The Prophet ﷺ supplicated,

> O Allah, place light in my heart, light in my tongue, light in my hearing, light in my sight, light behind me, light in front of me, light on my right, light on my left, light above me and light below me. Place light in my sinew, in my flesh, in my blood, in my hair and in my skin. Place light in my soul and make light abundant for me. Make me light and grant me light.

Maymuna was always good natured, pleasant with everyone and lived in harmony with all the Prophet's other wives. She was married to the Prophet ﷺ for the last three years of his life and narrated sixty-seven hadiths. Maymuna lived for another forty years or more, which were full of devotion, piety and loyalty to the Prophet's memory. She performed Hajj every year, yet in her final Hajj, she became ill on her way from Mecca back to Medina and died in Sarif, the very place where she had consummated her marriage with the Prophet ﷺ.

At her funeral, her nephew, Ibn Abbas said, "This is the wife of the Messenger of Allah ﷺ, so when you lift her bier, do not shake her, be gentle with her - she is your mother." Aisha also said, "Oh, Maymuna passed away. By Allah, she was pious and kept good terms with her kin." Maymuna died at the age of eighty in 51 AH. May Allah bless the blessed mother of the believers.

MARIA AL-QIBTIYA

Maria al-Qibtiya, or Mary the Copt, was born in upper Egypt to a Coptic father and Greek mother. When Maria was still young, she was given to the court of Muqawqis, the Patriarch of Alexandria. He held religious and political leadership over the Egyptian Copts even though the Romans were occupying Egypt.

After the treaty of Hudaybiya and following the consolidation of power over Mecca and Medina by the first Muslims, the Prophet ﷺ dispatched emissaries bearing letters to the great kings and leaders of the Middle East, inviting them to Islam. Muqawqis was among the recipients. He graciously received the Prophet's envoy, Hatib ibn abi Balta'a, who was well known for his eloquence and wisdom. He hosted him, read the letter and while he accepted the prophethood of Muhammad ﷺ, he did not accept the message of Islam for himself, saying he could not compromise his sovereignty. But he honoured the Prophet ﷺ by sending gifts back with the envoy, which included twenty fine cloths, gold, a eunuch known as Ma'boor and, most importantly, he sent Maria and her sister, Sirin. Hatib noticed the anxiety in the two women's faces on their way to Medina, so he began telling them about the history of Medina and the status of Muslims. He told them about Islam in great depth and soon after his elegant explanation of the faith, they embraced Islam.

Maria was a beautiful woman with a fair complexion and curly hair. The Prophet ﷺ admired her grace and chose Maria for himself, while giving her sister Sirin to the great poet, Thabit al-Ansari.

Maria's arrival made Aisha jealous. She could see how beautiful Maria was and how caring the Prophet ﷺ was towards her. Aisha said,

> I have never been jealous of any woman as I have been of Maria. This is because she was beautiful and curly-haired. The Messenger of Allah ﷺ was fond of her. When she first arrived, the Prophet ﷺ lodged her at the house of Haritha ibn Numan. She became our neighbour. He would stay with her day and night until we prepared a room for her in the Prophet's house. However, she was afraid, and so the Prophet ﷺ moved her to the upper room where he would frequently visit her. And that would terribly upset us.

Once, the Prophet ﷺ took Maria to Hafsa's house while she was visiting her father and when she returned, she was distressed to find them alone together in her home. Hafsa complained bitterly to the Prophet ﷺ and in trying to appease her, he said, "Will it not please you if I forbid her for myself and not come near her again?" She answered, "Yes." So the Prophet ﷺ promised he would not approach Maria, as long as Hafsa kept this secret to herself. But she could not contain the secret and told it to some of the other wives. Allah then revealed these verses,

> The Prophet told something in confidence to one of his wives. When she disclosed it [to another wife] and God made this known to him, he confirmed part of it, keeping the rest to himself. When he confronted

her with what she had done, she asked, "Who told you about this?" and he replied, "The All Knowing, the All Aware told me." If both of you [wives] repent to God, for your hearts have deviated, [all will be well]. If you collaborate against him, [be warned that] God will aid him, as will Jibril and all righteous believers and the angels too will back him." (Quran 66:3–5)

Maria was tested again when she was accused of indecency by the hypocrites, who said that they saw a man coming out of her house very often, who visited her when she was alone. Umar saw how upset the Prophet ﷺ was and, taking up his sword, went directly to the apartment of Maria while the man was still with her. He went to strike him, but it was Maria's relative, the eunuch who had come with her from Alexandria.

Ibn Abdul Hakam narrated the account, on the authority of Abdullah ibn Umar who said,

> The eunuch exposed himself for he had no genitals. When Umar saw that, he returned to the Messenger of Allah and informed him of what he saw. The Prophet thereupon said, "Angel Jibril has come to me and informed me that Allah has exonerated Maria and her relative and that she is pregnant of a son for me and that he resembles me more than anybody else. He also commanded me to name him Ibrahim and he [Jibril] called me Abu Ibrahim".

Before Maria fell pregnant, the Prophet ﷺ had told her the story of Hajar ؏, Ibrahim's wife, who had come to the Hijaz centuries before, far from her home. He pointed out parallels between Maria and Hajar. Maria said they did indeed have similarities, except Hajar had a son, while she did not. But a year after her arrival in Mecca, Maria became pregnant. The Prophet ﷺ was overjoyed at the prospect of a child. He had lost all his sons and daughters except Fatima al-Zahra ؏.

Maria gave birth to a beautiful boy who resembled the Prophet ﷺ. He named him Ibrahim after the Prophet Ibrahim, as the angel Jibril ؏ had instructed. Maria's son was a significant blessing in her life, as he also brought her freedom. She was no longer a slave, following the Islamic legal rule concerning bondswomen that those who bear children would be freed as soon as they gave birth. The Messenger of Allah ﷺ said about Maria, "Her son has set her free." The Prophet's affection for the mother of his new son increased even further. He visited Maria and Ibrahim incessantly, playing with his son, holding him close to his chest and loving him dearly as a devoted father.

However, little Ibrahim's life was not destined to see beyond eighteen months. He fell ill with a fever and never recovered. He was taken back to Allah ten years after the Hijra. Anas ﷺ said,

> I saw Ibrahim dying in the Prophet's arms. The Prophet's eyes filled with tears and he said, "O Ibrahim, if it were not that the promise of reunion is sure and that this is a path that all must tread and that the last of us should overtake the first, truly we should grieve for you with yet a greater sorrow. Yet we are stricken indeed with grief for you, O Ibrahim. The eyes shed tears and the heart grieves. We only say what pleases Allah."

The Prophet ﷺ led the funeral prayer and the women wept in solidarity with the Messenger of Allah. Maria, her heart filled with grief, patiently repeated the words that her noble husband had taught her, "We belong to Allah and to Him we shall return". The Prophet ﷺ comforted Maria, saying that Ibrahim was now in Paradise and would have two angels breastfeeding him until he was two years old.

Soon after the burial of tiny Ibrahim, there was an eclipse of the sun. Thereupon some people said, "The sun eclipsed for the death of Ibrahim!" But this was coincidental. When the Messenger of Allah heard what they said, he quickly declared, "The sun and the moon are two of the signs of Allah. They do not eclipse because of anyone's death or because of their life."

Maria lived for five years after the death of Allah's Messenger ﷺ. Abu Bakr used to financially support her and Umar continued to support her after Abu Bakr. Maria had been a loving wife and a deeply patient woman who endured difficult tests, most heartbreaking of all the loss of her beloved son, Ibrahim. After losing her son and her husband, Maria left this world in the month of Muharram in 637, sixteen years after the Hijra. Umar gathered people to attend her funeral and led the funeral prayer, and she was buried along with the other mothers of the believers. May Allah grant peace and ease to Maria al-Qibtiya, the mother of Ibrahim.

MUHAMMAD, THE HUSBAND

"The best of you is the one who is best to his wife, and I am the best of you to my wives." (Tirmidhi and Ibn Majah)

Having recounted the noble lives of the mothers of the believers ﷺ, it is important to emphasise how they helped shape the legacy of their blessed husband, the Messenger of Allah ﷺ. It is through them that we have access to the most intimate details of the Prophet's life and characteristics, especially in his blueprint as an exceptional husband. For he treated his wives with kindness, justice, compassion and affection and distributed his time with equity.

We hear through Aisha how the Prophet ﷺ helped in the household with tasks; he milked his goat, mended his own clothes and tended to his wives' needs. Aisha narrates, "He did what one of you would do in his house. He mended sandals and patched garments and sewed" ('*Adab al-Mufrad*' graded *sahih* by al-Albani). Aisha was once asked, "What did the Prophet ﷺ do in his house?" She replied, "He used to keep himself busy serving his family and when it was the time for prayer, he would go for it" (Bukhari).

As a point of clarity, the word used in the hadith, "*mihnah*" (مِهنة) or "busy serving", also means work, job or profession. This indicates that housework is a job and that it is the Sunnah for husbands to undertake work in the household, following the example of the best of husbands.

The mothers of the believers were also the best of wives. They are excellent examples for both men and women throughout the centuries in regard to their integrity, intelligence and piety. All were brilliant students, and the Prophet ﷺ imparted his knowledge to them every morning, while the evening was reserved for their pleasure and intimate enjoyment. They came from different races, ages and personalities, and the Prophet ﷺ honoured each of their unique characters and nature. Quite simply, in them we see role models and the etiquettes of marriage through their relationship with the Prophet ﷺ.

THE GOOD-HUMOURED HUSBAND

The Prophet ﷺ was incredibly kind, affectionate and humorous with his wives. He made them laugh, smiled at them and used to embrace them in his arms. They also brought him joy, as we saw with Sawda bint Zama ﷺ, who made him laugh until his teeth were visible.

There were also many tender moments between the Prophet ﷺ and his wives that demonstrated his considerate manner towards them. Aisha, the mother of the believers ﷺ, said,

> By Allah, I saw the Prophet ﷺ standing at the door of my room screening me with his garment to enable me to watch the Abyssinians playing with spears in the mosque. I placed my head between his ear and shoulder and my face was leaning against his cheek. Then he said, "O Aisha, are you satisfied?" I replied, "No" so that I might know how dear I am to him. He asked me repeatedly until I became satisfied. (Bukhari)

In another version, she said, "He was standing especially for me until I became bored and left. Therefore, you should treat a girl who is fond of amusement (providing that it is permissible) according to her age." The Prophet ﷺ ensured there was time for his wives to enjoy life, so they would not find marriage boring or difficult. Aisha said,

> Once I travelled with Allah's Messenger ﷺ when I was young and light. He asked his Companions to go ahead and they did so. Afterwards he said, "Let us race each other." I ran and I won. Later on, when I became fat and forgot what had happened, I travelled again with him. He asked his Companions to go ahead and they did so. Then he said, "Let us race each other." I had forgotten what had happened in the first race. I was fat and I said, "O Messenger of Allah, how can I race you?" But he said, "Let us race." We raced and when he won, he started to laugh and said, "this one was for that one."

The Messenger of Allah ﷺ was also playful and knew when Aisha was annoyed at him, saying to her, "I know when you are angry and when you are pleased with me." She said, "How could you know that?" He said, "When you are pleased, you say, 'No, by the Lord of Muhammad' and when you are angry, you say, 'No, by the Lord of Ibrahim' " (Bukhari).

The Prophet ﷺ was always patient with his wives and never treated them with harshness, even when they argued with him. Once, when Umar's wife ؓ argued with him, he said, "Do you argue with me?" She answered, "The Prophet's wives argue with him and he is better than you."

This was the Prophet's way with his wives. He was considerate, kind and wanted them to embrace the innocent joys of married life. His manner, character and affection always enriched the love between them and all his marriages provide us with a beautiful example of domestic harmony.

THE SERIOUS HUSBAND

While the Prophet ﷺ treated his wives kindly and was funny around them and patient with their mistakes, he was also serious and decisive when the situation required it. One time, when some of the mothers of the believers complained to the Prophet ﷺ and asked for an easier life filled with more luxuries, the Prophet ﷺ could not submit to their demands. Even though they knew he ﷺ had to set an example to his community of believers, they asked for something he could not give them and he swore that he would not approach them for a month. Then Allah the Almighty addressed Muhammad ﷺ by saying, "Prophet, say to your wives, 'If your desire is for the present life and its finery, then come, I will make provision for you and release you with kindness, but if you desire God, His Messenger, and the Final Home, then remember that God has prepared great rewards for those of you who do good.' " (Quran 33:28–29)

The Prophet ﷺ went to speak with them, beginning with Aisha. He said, "O Aisha, I would like to offer you something, but it is best for you to consult your parents and not to be rash." She asked, "What is it, Messenger of Allah ﷺ?" He then recited the verses. She said, "Would I consult my parents concerning you? I would rather choose Allah, His

Messenger and the Final Home." She added, "I wish that you would not inform any of your other wives with what I said." He said, "If any of them asks, I will tell her. Allah did not send me to be harsh, but he sent me as a teacher."

He gave his wives a choice. They could divorce him in kindness from him and enjoy the glitter of this world or stay with him and sacrifice it all. The wives understood their mistake and the gravity of the Prophet's responsibilities and chose to remain his wives and submit to Allah. They lived with the Prophet ﷺ and committed themselves to carrying out their great roles in the best possible way. The Prophet ﷺ only acted in wisdom and fairness to his community, he could not give more to his wives when others suffered. His commitment to his faith, justice and humility was something he wanted his wives to share in so that together they would be enduring examples to the early Muslims and to believers throughout time and place.

THE FAITHFUL HUSBAND

Prophet Muhammad's commitment and loyalty to his wives was paramount, he ensured their rights were fulfilled and gave them respect, honour and love. We see no greater example of the Prophet's ﷺ faithfulness than in his loyalty to his first wife Khadija ﷺ. When Khadija died, the Prophet ﷺ kept her memory alive all his life. She never left his heart, so much so that anyone connected to Khadija was treated with nothing but the utmost respect and kindness from him. Aisha narrates, "Once an old woman visited the Prophet ﷺ. He asked her, 'Who are you?' She replied, 'Juthama al-Mazaniyya.' He said, 'Then you are Hassana! How are you? And how have you been?' The woman said, 'I sacrifice my father and mother for you.' " When she left, Aisha asked him about the woman - she wanted to know the reason for his hospitality towards her. The Prophet ﷺ told her that she often used to visit during the life of Khadija. He added, "Loyalty is of belief."

Aisha ﷺ also said,

> I was never jealous of any of the Prophet's wives ﷺ except Khadija because the Prophet ﷺ frequently remembered her. One day he remembered her and I said, "What do you need with an old woman

when Allah favoured you with someone better than her [meaning herself]?" The Prophet ﷺ said, "No, by Allah! He has not given me better than her. She believed in me when the people disbelieved. When they called me a liar, she alone remained true. She enriched me when the people deprived me. Allah has favoured her in that she gave me offspring, and I was granted children from no one else."

Such kind treatment to Khadija in her lifetime and after her death indicates the Prophet's noble morals, deep affection and lasting devotion. Through the narrations of accounts of his blessed wives ﷺ, Prophet Muhammad ﷺ will always remain a beacon of light and love for spouses the world over.

THE PROPHET'S DAUGHTERS

ZAYNAB

Zaynab was Muhammad's first child of his first love, Khadijah bint Khuwaylid. Zaynab was born ten years before the Prophet received the first revelation. As the daughter of such excellent and noble parents, Zaynab was a model of virtue and honour and grew up in a household filled with harmony and love.

When Zaynab was old enough for marriage, her cousin Abu al-As ibn al-Rabia asked for her hand in marriage. He descended from Abdul Manaf ibn Qusay, the Prophet's grandfather, and from the maternal side, he descended from Khuwaylid, Khadija's father. Despite his young age, he was one of the leading merchants of the Quraysh. His wisdom and good character commanded the respect of the people and their elders.

Abu al-As was very close to his aunt Khadija, who treated him like her own son. He often visited his aunt's house and every time he saw Zaynab, he was taken by her beauty, gentleness and good nature. Zaynab was also at ease in his presence and loved to listen to his speeches and his jokes. Naturally, their two hearts opened to one another.

When Abu al-As asked for Zaynab's hand in marriage, Prophet Muhammad received him well and listened to him attentively but said he would ask his daughter's opinion. He went to Zaynab and told her, "Daughter, your cousin, Abu al-As ibn al-Rabia, is interested in you." Zaynab kept quiet out of shyness, and she did not utter a word. But her face became red and she shut her eyes. The Messenger of Allah smiled and did not repeat the question, for he understood what was in her heart. He then went back to Abu al-As and shook his hand in congratulations and then made a supplication to bless their union.

Zaynab and Abu al-As were about to embark on a great love story, one that would be met with challenges and demonstrate their devotion to one another. But first, they began their married life with happiness and harmony. Zaynab gave birth to two children who brought even more joy and delight into their home, a son called Ali and a daughter called Umama ؉ – the Prophet's first grandchildren.

As a trader, Abu al-As travelled a great deal and would be away in Syria for many days, during which time Zaynab missed him immensely. One time, when Abu al-As was travelling, a pivotal event in human history took place - Muhammad ؉ was appointed as a messenger of mercy to all the worlds. Zaynab immediately responded to the call that was placed upon her father, and she readily embraced Islam. Abu al-As returned from his journey and discovered that his wife had accepted the new faith. She tried to convince him to embrace Islam, but she could not turn his heart. He justified his refusal by saying, "By Allah, I have nothing against your father, and nothing is dearer to me than following the same path with you, my love. But I hate that people should say that I have disappointed my clan by disbelieving in the deities of my ancestors in order to please my wife. Can you please excuse me?" Zaynab was unsettled by his disbelief. Their household, that had been one of love and unity, was suddenly tinged with tension and anxiety, but Zaynab did not leave her husband. The Quraysh leaders also put pressure on Abu al-As to divorce his wife. They hoped to entice him by promising him the richest and most beautiful woman as a wife should he divorce Zaynab, but he replied, "I love my wife deeply and passionately and I have great and high esteem for her father even though I have not entered the religion of Islam."

The following years saw the persecution of the early Muslims by the Quraysh, during which Zaynab's dear mother, the Lady Khadija, died and her father and sisters migrated to Medina, while she remained in Mecca. Zaynab cried and cried and resigned her fate to Allah, hoping that He would one day provide a way out for all of them.

Afterwards, in the battle of Badr, Abu al-As was taken as a prisoner of war. The Prophet ؉ asked the Muslims to treat the prisoners kindly. Meanwhile, Zaynab sent some money and a necklace to ransom her husband. The necklace was a wedding present from her mother. No sooner did the Prophet ؉ see this necklace than he remembered his loyal wife Khadija and his heart was filled with compassion. After a long silence, the Prophet ﷺ said, "If you would like to release her prisoner and give her back her money, you may do so." They all said, "Yes, Messenger of Allah." Then, it was time for Abu al-As to release Zaynab from marriage. The Prophet ﷺ took a pledge from him, saying that Islam put a barrier between them.

When Abu al-As returned to Mecca, Zaynab was elated to see him, but she saw sadness in his eyes. He told her that he had come to bid her farewell, and deeply saddened, Zaynab asked, "Where are you going and why?" He replied, "You are going, not me. I promised your father to return you to him, because Islam puts a barrier between us. And I have never broken a promise." Zaynab reluctantly departed Mecca and bade Abu al-As an emotional farewell. He told her, "Zaynab, whatever happens, I shall always love you as long as I live. Your ghost shall forever continue to fill this house that has witnessed the sweetest and the most pleasant days of our life." Wiping away her tears, Zaynab left for Medina to join her father and sisters.

But then something happened on the way to Medina. Some members of the Quraysh obstructed Zaynab, terrifying her until she fell from her camel. She was pregnant at the time and suffered a miscarriage. She returned to Mecca under the shelter and protection of Abu al-As, and he took great care of her until she regained her health and strength.

Once she was recovered, Abu al-As would not let her leave alone again. He accompanied her, along with his brother, Kinana ibn al-Rabia, and they took her to the Prophet ﷺ in Medina. Each lived without the other in Mecca and Medina and while the years passed by, Zaynab fervently hoped that Allah would open the heart of Abu al-As to Islam.

After six years, in the dead of night, there was a knock on Zaynab's door. It was Abu al-As. He had been travelling back from Syria with a Quraysh caravan, when Zayd ibn al-Haritha, along with 170 riders sent by the Prophet ﷺ accosted the caravan. They returned to Medina taking those who were guarding the caravan as captives. Abu al-As escaped and sought refuge in the house of his former wife. She could not believe her eyes when she saw him at her door. She was eager to greet him but checked herself.

Abu al-As said, "I did not come to Medina as a warrior, I come as a merchant. Nevertheless, a squad belonging to your father obstructed us and robbed my caravan as spoils of war. But I managed to escape. I came to you seeking your intercession on my part to the Muslims." Zaynab said, "Welcome, my cousin. Welcome, father of Ali and Umamah." She went forward to the Prophet ﷺ after he had performed the dawn prayer and exclaimed, "O people, I have given protection to Abu al-As ibn al-Rabia!"

Then the Prophet ﷺ went out and said, "O people, did you hear what I heard?" They replied, "Yes, Messenger of Allah." Then he said, "I swear by Him in Whose Hand is my life, I knew nothing of this matter until I heard what you have also heard now." And he added, "The Muslims are like one hand against those who are outside their community and the lowest of the Muslims is entitled to give protection on behalf of the rest of his co-Muslims. So we give protection to whom she has given protection."

Then the Messenger of Allah ﷺ went to his daughter's home and said, "Be hospitable towards him, but do not be alone with him - you are not lawful to him." Zaynab asked her father ﷺ to give Abu al-As his property back. The Prophet ﷺ, out of love for her and mercy to Abu al-As, went to his Companions and said, "You know this man, whose property you took. I would like to give him back his property." The Prophet ﷺ did not order them but gave his Companions a choice, "But if you do not like to do that, it will be your booty given to you by Allah." They all replied, "We would like to give it back, Messenger of Allah."

Abu al-As reflected on Zaynab's love for him, his undying love for her and on the beauty of Islam to which she held so steadfast, sacrificing their life together. It dawned on him that he had been living in ignorance, and he decided he wanted to embrace the truth. But he did not want anyone to think he embraced Islam due to pressure or influence. And so, Abu al-As bid farewell to Zaynab and set out for Mecca. Having arrived there with his prosperous caravan, he began to give back what he had taken from people. Then he stood in front of the Quraysh and said, "O people of Quraysh, is there anyone to whom I still owe a debt?" They replied, "No, you are loyal and generous." Then he declared, "I testify that there is no god but Allah, and Muhammad is the Messenger of Allah. By Allah, I wanted to embrace Islam before now, but I feared that you might say that I wanted to misappropriate your property. But when Allah helped me to give it back to you, I embraced Islam."

Abu al-As returned to Medina and joined the Muslim community. There the Prophet ﷺ returned Zaynab to him and their marriage was renewed. The couple were overjoyed to be together again and lived in blissful happiness, united in love and faith. But their reunion was to be short-lived. Zaynab, who had been suffering from complications of haemorrhage since her fall in the first attempted migration to Medina, died a year later, in the fifth year after Hijra.

Abu al-As was devastated and cried so many tears at her funeral that he caused everyone around him to weep. Then the Prophet ﷺ came to bid farewell to his daughter. His eyes were full of tears and his heart full of sorrow. The grief held a double sting for him, as Zaynab's death reminded him of the death of her mother, his darling wife Khadija ﷺ. The Prophet ﷺ said to the women performing the ritual bathing of Zaynab, "Wash her three times and let the last wash be mixed with camphor oil." After they washed her, he prayed over his beloved daughter's body. May Allah be pleased with Zaynab, the first child of the Messenger of Allah ﷺ.

RUQAYYA

When Ruqayya was born three years after Zaynab, she was a huge source of happiness to her parents Prophet Muhammad ﷺ and Khadija ﷺ who lavished her with love. They were soon to be blessed with further joy through a third daughter, Umm Kulthum. At a time when baby girls were undesired and even buried alive for their gender, it is even more poignant how much the Prophet ﷺ and Khadija cherished and loved their daughters, whom they saw as nothing less than miraculous gifts from Allah.

Ruqayya and Umm Kulthum were so close in age that they were brought up together like they were twin sisters. They had a deep bond, a unique closeness and shared everything in life, even the manner of their marriages. When the two sisters had reached maturity, Abu Talib went to the Prophet ﷺ with proposals on behalf of his brother's sons. Abdul-Uzza ibn Abdul Muttalib, also known as Abu Lahab, had two sons, Utbah and Utaybah, who wished to marry the Prophet's two daughters. The proposals came at a time when Muhammad ﷺ was not yet appointed as a messenger of Islam.

Abu Talib said, "We came to ask for the hands of our daughters,

Ruqayya and Umm Kulthum, in marriage. We hope that you will not make their marriage difficult to your cousins, Utba and Utayba, sons of Abdul-Uzza." The Prophet ﷺ asked his uncle to grant him time to consult his wife and daughters. When he told Khadija about the proposals, Khadija ؓ fell silent for some time. She knew that Umm Jamil, the wife of Abu Lahab and the mother of Utba and Utayba, was a hard-hearted, pompous and sharp-tongued woman. Khadija was concerned about her daughters entering the home of such a harsh mother-in-law. But she did not wish to break her husband's ties of kinship with his family, so she did not speak out against the marriages. The two girls also kept silent out of shyness.

The Prophet ﷺ decided to proceed with their marriages, and the wedding contracts took place in an atmosphere tainted with anxiety. Ruqayya and Umm Kulthum's affectionate father invoked blessings on his daughters and left them in the care of Allah. It was soon after their marriages that Muhammad ﷺ received the light of the first revelation and began to call the Meccans to Islam. The people of Quraysh, including Abu Lahab, gathered together to conspire against him. Khadija worried for her daughters, being at the mercy of Abu Lahab and Umm Jamil.

One of the Qurashi people told Abu Lahab, "You took charge of Muhammad's responsibilities. You should return his daughters to him." Abu Lahab then warned his two sons, "I will deprive you of my fatherhood, if you do not divorce Muhammad's two daughters." They obeyed their father and divorced their wives before the consummation of the marriage took place. The two young ladies returned to their father's house in great distress.

Abu Lahab and his wife Umm Jamil cruelly opposed the Prophet ﷺ to the point of incurring Allah's curse upon them, as the Quran states, "May the hands of Abu Lahab be ruined! May he be ruined too! Neither his wealth nor his gains will help him" (Quran 111:1–2). Abu Lahab took every opportunity to attack the Prophet ﷺ. He abused and insulted him with no regard whatsoever for their blood relations. Umm Jamil used to collect thorns and throw them upon the Messenger's path. "The time of sleep is over, O Khadija," the Prophet exclaimed to his loving wife. The bitter persecution and prejudice against the Muslims intensified, especially against the weaker among the fledgling community.

Ruqayya bore these hardships patiently along with her father. After being dishonoured by Abu Lahab's son in his divorce of her, she was destined to marry one of the best of men – Uthman ibn Affan ibn Abi al-As. Uthman was one of the first eight people to enter Islam and one of the ten who were informed that they would enter Paradise. He was later to become one of the rightly guided caliphs.

Uthman was one of the most respected Quraysh youths in terms of lineage, prestige and wealth. The Quraysh mothers used to sing a lullaby for their children about him, saying, "By Allah, I love you as the Quraysh love Uthman." When the Messenger of Allah ﷺ gave his daughter, Ruqayyah, to Uthman in marriage, the lullaby changed to, "The best two people who met each other were Ruqayyah and her husband Uthman."

Al-Zubayr reported that the Messenger of Allah ﷺ sent a man with a gift to Uthman and Ruqayya. The man then came back late. The Messenger of Allah ﷺ told the man, "Do you want me to inform you about what delayed you?" The man answered in the affirmative. The Prophet ﷺ then said, "You stood there looking at Uthman and Ruqayyah admiring their beauty."

When the Prophet ﷺ permitted his Companions to leave for Abyssinia, the newlywed Uthman and Ruqayya were among the emigrants. Ruqayya hugged her father, mother and sisters, almost choking with sorrow and distress at having to part with them. Uthman also looked downcast. Ruqayya saw his grave face and reassured her husband, "Allah is indeed with us and with those we are leaving behind in the vicinity of the Ancient House."

After reaching Abyssinia, Ruqayya and Uthman lived in peace, but always lived in hope to return to Mecca and be with the Prophet ﷺ and his Companions. As soon as they heard that Hamza and Umar had embraced Islam, they began their journey back, thinking things must have improved. But as soon as they set foot in Mecca, they were shocked to see that the polytheists' persecution had only increased. Yet Ruqayya was about to face another personal and tragic blow. When she entered her father's house, she learned that her beloved mother Khadija ﷺ had died. Ruqayya could not stop weeping, but she accepted His decree and placed her trust and fate entirely in Allah's Hands. Uthman and Ruqayya did not stay long in Mecca. They migrated to Medina once the Ansar (the Aws and Khazraj tribes) had pledged allegiance to Muhammad ﷺ. Ruqayya became known as the "lady of two emigrations".

In Medina, Ruqqaya gave birth to her only child who they named Abdullah. After enduring years of hardship, Ruqayya and Uthman's son filled his parents' lives with happiness. But they were to be tested yet again. One day, while Abdullah was sleeping in his cradle, a rooster appeared and pecked at his eyes. This led to an infection that claimed his life a few days later. Ruqayya's heart was broken in two, and she contracted a terrible fever. Her loving husband stayed by the side of his wife nursing her and begging Allah to alleviate her suffering and make her recover from her illness. While he was nursing his sick wife, he heard the voice of the announcer calling on the emigrants and the Ansar to help accost the caravan of the Quraysh that was on its way back from Syria. Uthman felt he must go and do his duty, but the Prophet ﷺ commanded him to remain close by his sick wife to care for her until she recovered.

But Ruqayya was never to recover. Her disease was so severe that it claimed her life. At the same time that the bereaved Uthman kissed his wife's forehead and fingertips, proclamations could be heard outside announcing the Muslims' victory. The Messenger of Allah ﷺ was distraught at the news of his daughter's death. He moved closer to her side and sorrowfully bade her farewell. Fatima, the Prophet's other daughter, stood by Ruqayya's deathbed, weeping for her dear sister. The Prophet ﷺ helped her to her feet and gently wiped her tears away with his garment. The bereaved father ﷺ performed the funeral prayers for his daughter and followed her body to the place of burial. And so ended the life of the patient and pious Ruqayya, may Allah be pleased with the daughter of Muhammad ﷺ.

UMM KULTHUM

Umm Kulthum was born shortly after Ruqayya and became an excellent companion to her sister. As stated before, they were raised like twins. Even their betrothals to Abu Lahab's two sons took place at the same time. After their marriages to Utbah and Utaybah were dissolved, Umm Kulthum's sister Ruqayya married Uthman ﷺ and they emigrated together to Abyssinia.

Umm Kulthum, along with her younger sister Fatima, stayed in Mecca to witness the severest period of persecution against her father and the early Muslims. Umm Kulthum, taking the mantle of the eldest daughter, tried her best to help in the household affairs and to relieve the Prophet's grief at the cruel rejection of the Meccan pagans. Things were about to become even worse. The people of the Quraysh decided to strike an economic and social boycott against the Muslims and Banu Hashim. Umm Kulthum, along with her family and the early band of Muslims, were driven out of their homes to mete out a life in the valley of Abu Talib. Here, exposed to the harsh environment, they suffered starvation, isolation and extreme hardship for years. Umm Kulthum endured the afflictions of the siege and the pains of hunger side by side with her father and the Muslim community.

They survived on leaves and even dirt. Sa'd ibn Abi said, "I had suffered hunger so much so that one night, I trampled upon something that was succulent and I put it in my mouth and swallowed it though I did not know what that thing was." According to some narrations, he had eaten animal droppings.

Sometimes food was smuggled to them, especially by some Meccans who had relatives among those driven to the valley. Hisham ibn Amr ibn Rabia al-Amiri was one of those pained by the injustice that the Muslims were suffering. He loaded a camel with food every night and released it at the valley's entrance. The camel would then appear to the starving Muslims as if it were a miracle sent from the heaven. But other attempts to bring them relief were thwarted. Abu Jahl noticed that Khadija's nephew, Hakim ibn Hizam ibn Khuwaylid, was secretly carrying wheat to the valley. Abu Jahl caught him and shouted, "Are you carrying food to Banu Hashim? By Allah! I will not allow you and your food to leave here until I expose you in Mecca!"

Umm Kulthum cared as well as she could for her father, her younger sister and her mother, who was very ill and weak. Finally, after three long years, the oppressive boycott ended. But it took its toll on the noble Khadija. Her disease grew fatal, and she tragically died, leaving her family heartbroken. Umm Kulthum then shouldered the responsibility of managing the Prophet's household affairs.

Later on, when the Quraysh plotted to assassinate the Prophet ﷺ, Muhammad ﷺ ordered the Muslims to emigrate to Medina. He and Abu Bakr left Mecca together in secret. But the Prophet's daughters, Umm Kulthum and Fatima, remained in Mecca for their safety. After the Prophet ﷺ reached Medina, he sent Zayd ibn al-Haritha to bring his daughters to him from Mecca. Umm Kulthum and her sister bade farewell at their mother's grave and headed for their new home.

In Medina, Umm Kulthum finally enjoyed a life of peace and contentment. Her dear sister Ruqayya also returned to the family and lived in happiness in Medina, witnessing her father gain victory against the oppressive Quraysh. After having to endure terrible suffering during the boycott, Umm Kulthum's heart lifted in joy to see the return of her father victorious from the Battle of Badr.

But soon after that, Ruqayya, her beloved twin-like sister, suddenly died. Three years passed and Umm Kulthum's heart was still shadowed in sorrow for the loss of her sister. She saw how Ruqayya's grieving husband, Uthman, would often come to her father to receive condolence, advice and support over the death of his precious wife. She saw how the tears rolled down his cheeks in grief. One day, Umar ibn al-Khattab ؓ came complaining to the Prophet ﷺ that both Abu Bakr and Uthman refused his offer to marry his daughter, Hafsa. The Prophet ﷺ said to him, "Hafsa will marry someone who is better than Uthman, and Uthman will marry someone better than Hafsa." Then, the Prophet ﷺ addressed Uthman saying, "I am giving you Umm Kulthum, Ruqayyah's sister, in marriage. If I had ten daughters, I would have married them to you in succession." And so Umm Kulthum married the noble Uthman and he earned the title, "the possessor of the two lights" because he had been married to two cherished daughters of the blessed Prophet Muhammad ﷺ.

Umm Kulthum lived happily with Uthman for the next six years. She witnessed her husband's beautiful, selfless and generous character and how he supported and fought valiantly for Islam. In the month of Dhul-Qadah in 6 AH, the Messenger of Allah ﷺ set out on his camel, leading about 1,500 Muslims towards Mecca to perform Umrah, but the Quraysh stopped them from entering the city. The Muslims had reached Hudaybiya and the Messenger of Allah ﷺ told his son-in-law Uthman, "Go to the Quraysh and tell them that we have not come to fight anyone. We only came to visit the House, honouring its sacredness and bringing with us the sacrifice. And we shall leave."

When Uthman did not return for a long time, a rumour spread that he had been killed by the Quraysh. Umm Kulthum wept and trembled in fear that her beloved husband might be harmed. Her love for Uthman had grown deep, as had his love for her. But to her joy and relief, he returned safely. The Prophet ﷺ then ordered everyone to sacrifice their animals and shave their hair. When Umm Kulthum heard her father, the Messenger of Allah ﷺ say, "May Allah bless the shavers!" a cloud passed over her face, as she knew he ﷺ invoked blessings only upon the men. But the Prophet ﷺ, as astute as ever, brought a smile to his daughter's face when he added, "And those who cut their hair."

Two years later, after the conquest of Mecca in the year 8 AH, Umm Kulthum yearned to visit the grave of her mother, Khadija, but she never managed to pray over her mother's grave again, as Umm Kulthum died soon afterwards. The Messenger of Allah ﷺ buried her beside the remains of her beloved sister, Ruqayya. As in life, these two sisters were brought together in death, buried side by side. May Allah be pleased with the 'twin' sisters and beloved daughters of the Prophet ﷺ.

FATIMA AL-ZAHRA

Fatima al-Zahra bint Muhammad ﷺ was an individual of extraordinary and excellent character. She was strong, courageous and utterly devoted to Allah. She had a very special and beautiful bond with her father, Allah's messenger ﷺ. Fatima was the fourth daughter of the Prophet ﷺ and Khadija. She ﷺ was born at the time when her noble father had begun to seek out solitude in the mountains around Mecca, where he would meditate on the great mysteries of creation.

Fatima watched as her older sisters, who pampered and looked after her, got married and leave the family home. A dark cloud of sadness passed over the little girl. Fatima was inconsolable and her mother tenderly asked her why she wept so much. Fatima ﷺ said, "Do not allow anybody to take me away from you and my father. I cannot bear to leave you!" Her mother then smiled lovingly at her daughter and said gently said, "You will never leave us except if you wish to."

Fatima found some comfort in the friendship she had with Ali, her father's young cousin, who was only two years older than her and lived with them in the Prophet's house.

Yet when Fatima was five years old, a great event was about to occur that would change everything - her father was appointed as God's messenger to all of humanity. Her mother, Khadija, carefully explained to her young daughter what the Prophet ﷺ had to do. Fatima was an unusually sensitive child for her age. She drew even closer to her father ﷺ and grew in wisdom, loyalty and resilience alongside her father's mission. She would often be found walking courageously by his side through the narrow streets and alleys of Mecca, attending secret gatherings of the early Muslims who had pledged allegiance to the Prophet ﷺ or visiting the Holy Sanctuary.

One day, when she was not yet ten, she accompanied her father to the Kaaba, and he stood facing the holy precinct and began to pray. Fatima did not leave his side. A group from the Quraysh began to gather around him. Among them were the prominent pagan leaders Abu Jahl ibn Hishaam, Uqbah ibn Abi Muayt, Umayyah ibn Khalaf and Shaybah and Utbah. With cruel intent, the group moved closer to the Prophet ﷺ and Abu Jahl, the ringleader, sneered, "Which of you can bring the entrails of a slaughtered animal and throw it on Muhammad?"

Uqbah ibn Abi Muayt was only too eager and scurried off, returning with the filthy entrails and threw them on the blessed shoulders of the Prophet ﷺ while he was still prostrating. One of the Prophet's own companions, Abdullah ibn Masud, was fearful of the mighty Quraysh leaders and powerless to do or say anything.

But Fatima was enraged to see her father being so humiliated. This young girl, not even ten years old, promptly went straight up to her father and removed the offensive matter with her own hands. She then turned, stood firm and angrily rebuked the Qurayshi men. Astonished at her fearlessness, they did not speak a single word to her. When the Quraysh used to mock the Prophet ﷺ, they would say, "Muhammad has only daughters." Now they saw what a tower of strength his daughter could be.

Once the entrails were removed from his back, the noble Prophet ﷺ raised his head after the prostration and completed his prayer. He then said, "O Lord, may you punish the Quraysh!" and repeated this imprecation three times. Then he continued, "May You punish Utbah, Uqbah, Abu Jahl and Shaybah." These men, whom the Prophet ﷺ named, were all killed many years later at the Battle of Badr.

On another occasion, Fatima was with the Prophet ﷺ as he made *tawaf* (circumambulation) around the Kaaba. A Quraysh mob gathered around him, seized him and tried to strangle him with his own clothes. Fatima screamed and shouted for help. Abu Bakr heard her cries and came rushing to the scene and managed to free the Prophet ﷺ. While he was doing so, he pleaded, "Would you kill a man who says, 'My Lord is God?'" But the mob turned on Abu Bakr and began beating him until blood came flowing from his head and face. Thus was Fatima exposed to witnessing such violence and cruelty against her beloved father and the early Muslims. She did not retreat in fear or shyness but fought against the injustice like a true warrior.

Fatima's young life continued to be shaped with trials and challenges. She was one of the youngest members of the clans, at about twelve years old, when she suffered hunger and thirst along with her family in the valley of Abu Talib during the boycott. Three years later when it was lifted, Fatima was about to face the tragic loss of one of her parents. Fatima wept bitterly when her wonderful, caring mother Khadija passed away. Fatima was so heartbroken that her health deteriorated, some even feared she might die of grief.

However, Fatima knew she had to become even more resilient for her father, the noble Prophet ﷺ. She devoted herself to his care, giving him comfort and solace during every difficult moment. Fatima was so concerned for the Prophet's ﷺ welfare that she came to be called "Umm Abiha", the mother of her father.

She became so close to her father that often having to see him go through any trial was too much for her to bear. One time, an insolent mob had heaped dust and earth upon his gracious head, and when he returned home, Fatima saw the state her dear father was in and wept profusely while she wiped the dust from her father's head. "Do not cry, my daughter," he said, "for God shall protect your father."

The Prophet ﷺ had a deep and special bond with his beloved Fatima. He once said, "Whoever pleased Fatima has indeed pleased God and whoever has caused her to be angry has indeed angered God. Fatima is a part of me. Whatever pleases her, pleases me, and whatever angers her, angers me."

The Prophet's love and esteem for his daughter can be truly felt in his following words, "The best women in all the world are four: the Virgin Mary, Asiya - the wife of Pharoah, Khadijah - Mother of the Believers and Fatimah - daughter of Muhammad." Fatimah thus took a unique place in the Prophet's heart that was only occupied by his wife Khadija.

As well as being a woman of eloquence, wisdom and courage, Fatima ﷺ was deeply pious. She was given the title of "al-Zahra" which means "the resplendent one" because of her beaming face, which seemed to radiate light. It is said that when she stood for prayer, the *mihrab*, or prayer niche, would reflect the light of her countenance. She was also called "al-Batul" because of her asceticism. Instead of spending her time in the company of other women, much of it would be spent in ardent worship.

When the situation became worse than ever for the Muslims in Mecca, the Prophet ﷺ decreed that the emigration begin to Medina. Fatima and her sister, Umm Kulthum, stayed in Mecca until the Prophet ﷺ sent a Companion, Zayd ibn al-Haritha ﷺ, to bring them to their new home safely. When they finally arrived in Medina, they lived with their father in the simple dwelling he had built adjoining the mosque.

Fatima was then eighteen years old. Many of the great Companions asked for her hand in marriage, such as Abu Bakr and Umar, but the Prophet ﷺ graciously declined them. Then Ali ibn Abu Talib ﷺ managed to gather up some courage and went to the Prophet ﷺ to ask for Fatima's hand, hoping he could marry the girl with whom he had grown up. But when the humble and shy Ali was in the presence of the Prophet ﷺ, he became tongue-tied. He stared at the ground and could not speak one word. Ali was poor and overcome with nerves, he feared his proposal would be rejected.

The Messenger of Allah ﷺ looked at him with a smiling face and then asked, "What is the matter, son of Abu Talib?" Ali still could not speak and then the Prophet ﷺ gently said, "Perhaps you have come to propose marriage to Fatima?" Ali replied in a very low voice and with an extreme shyness, "Yes. I am asking for the hand of Fatima, daughter of Allah's Messenger in marriage." The Prophet ﷺ responded with a bright face saying, "Welcome!" Ali could hardly believe his ears. He took his leave with a happy heart and went outside to find a group of the Ansar eagerly waiting to hear what the Prophet ﷺ said. Ali told them, "I talked to the Messenger of Allah about the matter and he said, 'Welcome!' " The Prophet ﷺ then went in to tell his daughter that Ali had come forward to ask for her hand in marriage. Fatima shyly and silently accepted.

And so Fatima was to marry her friend, her relative and one of the dearest men to her father's heart. Ali had nothing to pay as a dowry but his shield, which had been a gift from the Prophet ﷺ to him. Ali sold his shield to Uthman in return for 470 dirhams. The Prophet ﷺ gave part of the money to Bilal to buy some perfume and gave the rest to Umm Salama to buy things for the new bride.

The Prophet ﷺ himself performed the marriage ceremony. At the *walima*, the guests were served with dates, figs and *hais* (a mixture of dates and butter fat). A leading member of the Ansar donated a ram and others made offerings of grain. It's also said that the Prophet's uncle, Hamza ﷺ, brought two rams and distributed their meat to the inhabitants of Medina. The entire city rejoiced in the union of Fatima and Ali ﷺ.

The Prophet ﷺ presented Fatima and Ali with the gift of a wooden bed intertwined with palm leaves, a velvet coverlet, a leather cushion filled with palm fibre, a sheepskin, a pot, a waterskin and a quern for grinding grain. After the Isha prayer, the Prophet ﷺ went to the bride and her groom. He asked for water, made ablution and poured the water upon them. He said, "O Allah, may you bless them, make blessing come upon them and bless their offspring."

Fatima and Ali had a very happy and beautiful marriage. They were poor, but she was content with her wonderful Ali, and together they were incredibly patient, becoming closer to each other with each passing day. Yet as the only one of her sisters who did not have a wealthy husband, Fatima felt the strain of household chores. She had no servants to help and had to grind corn herself until her hands cracked. Ali also worked to make ends meet. He spent his days filling heavy skins with water and carrying them to households. One day, Fatima said to Ali, "I have grinded until my hands are blistered." Ali said, "I have drawn water until I have pains in my chest." Ali went on to suggest to Fatima, "God has given your father some captives of war, go and ask him to give you a servant."

Reluctantly, she went to the Prophet ﷺ who said, "What has brought you here, my daughter?" She said, "I came to give you greetings of peace." She could not bring herself to ask of her father what was already difficult for him to give. Fatima returned home, telling her husband of her shame to ask her father for help. Ali went back to the Prophet ﷺ with Fatima, saying she was exhausted from work. Even though the Prophet's love for her was so immense, he could not show her favour over the poor and needy.

The Prophet ﷺ said, "By Allah, I will not give you what you ask while the people of Suffa (the poor who lived in the mosque) are tormented with hunger. I do not have enough for them." Ali and Fatima returned home feeling a little downcast, but that night, they heard the voice of the Prophet ﷺ asking permission to enter. They both began to rise to their feet to welcome him, but he said, "Stay where you are," and sat down beside them. He said, "Shall I not tell you of something better than that which you asked of me?" They replied, "Yes." The Prophet ﷺ continued, "It is a few words Jibril taught me: to glorify Allah [*subhanAllah*] ten times at the end of every prayer, to praise Allah [*alhamdulillah*] ten times and magnify Allah [*Allahu akbar*] ten times. When going to bed glorify Allah thirty-three times, praise Him thirty-three times and magnify Him thirty-three times. That is better than a servant." Ali used to say in later years, "I have never once failed to say them since the Messenger of God taught them to us."

One day, Ali and Fatima were fasting and prepared food mixed with butter to break their fast. The sun was on the verge of setting, and the couple were about to sit down to their iftar meal when they heard a knock at the door. Ali asked, "Who is it?" A voice answered, "A hungry and poor man." Ali and Fatima did not hesitate to give their food to the poor man, who thanked them and made supplications for them. Ali and Fatima broke their fast on only bread and water, entirely satisfied with what they had. On the following day, Ali and Fatima were about to break their fast when there was a knock on the door again. Ali asked, "Who is it?" A voice from outside replied, "An orphan who is displaced and starving." Ali did as he did the day before, giving their food to the orphan, and again, Fatima and Ali broke their fast on only bread and water, without any complaint. It happened again on the third day, and this time, the knock at the door came from a captive. Ali gave him their food, while he and his wife ate their meagre meal.

The three people who had come to the door were in fact all one and the same – it was the Angel Jibril ﷺ who manifested in different forms to test the faith and patience of Ali and Fatima. Jibril ﷺ informed the Messenger of Allah ﷺ of the incidents and gave him good tidings that Ali and Fatima would be rewarded with a carriage made of silver in Paradise.

Some *tafsir* scholars attribute this incident to the cause of the revelation of the following verses of the Quran, "They give food to the poor, the orphan and the captive, though they love it themselves, saying, 'We feed you for the sake of God alone seeking Allah's Countenance only. We seek neither recompense nor thanks from you' " (Quran 76:8–9). Such was the righteousness and generosity of Fatima and her husband Ali.

A year after they married, they were blessed with a baby boy, the Prophet's first grandson. The Prophet ﷺ was overjoyed. He recited the *adhan* in his tiny ear and named him al-Hasan, the beautiful one. The Prophet ﷺ softened a date between his lips and rubbed the newborn's mouth with its sweetness. He then shaved his grandson's hair and gave charity in a quantity equal to its weight in silver.

The following year, Fatima and Ali ﷺ were blessed with another son and called him al-Husayn, which means little Hasan or the little beautiful one. The Prophet ﷺ adored his grandsons. Fatima brought them to see the Prophet ﷺ as often as she could, knowing how fond he was of the beautiful boys. Their doting grandfather would take them to the mosque and when he prayed, they would playfully climb onto his back while he prostrated. The pure-hearted Prophet ﷺ would extend his prostration time so that his grandchildren could enjoy their play and safely get down before he raised his head, just as he did with his granddaughter Umama, the daughter of Zaynab.

Once, when the Prophet ﷺ was at Umm Salama's house, he called Fatima, al-Hasan and al-Husayn and covered them with his garment, saying, "O Allah! These are my household, O Allah! May you remove all abomination from them and make them pure and spotless." He repeated it three times. Then he said, "O Allah! May You make Your prayers and blessings be upon the household of Ibrahim. You are praiseworthy and glorious."

In the fifth year of the Hijra, Fatima and Ali were blessed yet again, this time with a daughter whom the Prophet ﷺ named Zaynab. Two years later, Fatima gave birth to a daughter whom the Prophet ﷺ called Umm Kulthum. He had lovingly named both his granddaughters in memory of their aunts, Fatima's sisters, who had passed away. And so the family of the Messenger of Allah ﷺ extended further through Fatima and Ali's children.

The bond between Fatima and her father only grew stronger. The love, the closeness, even Fatima's manner and character were a mirror of the Prophet ﷺ. Her intelligence and eloquence of speech was such that when she spoke, people would often be moved to tears, and their hearts filled with praise and gratitude to Allah. Aisha, the mother of the believers, said of her,

> I have not seen any one of God's creation resemble the Messenger of God more in speech, conversation and manner of sitting than Fatima, may God be pleased with her. When the Prophet saw her approaching, he would welcome her, stand up and kiss her, take her by the hand and sit her down in the place where he was sitting.

Fatima would also do the same when the Prophet ﷺ visited to her. She would stand up, joyously welcome him and kiss him. Whenever the Prophet ﷺ returned from a journey, he would pray two *rakahs* (units of prayer) in the mosque and then go to see Fatima before visiting any of his wives.

Amid his affection for her, the Prophet ﷺ was also keen to warn his daughter against anything that would displease Allah. He once said, "O Fatima bint Muhammad, save yourself from the Hellfire. It is not in my power to cause you harm or to bring you benefit beyond Allah's will" (Bukhari).

Thawban related that he once accompanied the Prophet ﷺ into Fatima's house. She was wearing a gold necklace that Ali had gifted her. This was at a time that funds were desperately needed to aid the Muslim campaigns, so the Prophet ﷺ could not bear to see any ostentation or display of wealth on his own family members, while the Muslims were struggling. The Prophet ﷺ said, "Fatima! Would you like it to be said that Fatima bint Muhammad had on a necklace of fire?" He left in disappointment. Fatima felt ashamed and sold the necklace, using the money to buy a slave and free her. When the Prophet ﷺ found out what she had done, he honoured the piety and wisdom of Fatima's actions. He said, "Praise be to Allah who saved Fatima from Hellfire" (Nasai).

Fatima played an active role in the growing Muslim community of Medina. Before her marriage, she selflessly tended to the poor and destitute who lived in the mosque. At times of battle, she was the first to care for her father and dress his wounds. During the Battle of the Ditch, she, together with other women, took the responsibility of preparing provisions during the long and difficult siege. In her camp, she led the Muslim women in prayer in a place upon which a mosque was built named 'Masjid Fatima', one of seven mosques where the Muslims stood guard and performed worship. Fatima had accompanied the Prophet ﷺ when he undertook Umrah after the Treaty of Hudaybiyyah. The following year, she and her sister Umm Kulthum, were among the mighty throng of Muslims who took part in the liberation of Mecca.

Fatima ؑ lived through trials and sorrows, joys and triumphs alongside the Prophet ﷺ. She had endured the bereavements of her mother Khadijah and her sisters Ruqayya, Zaynab and Umm Kulthum, one after the other. And now, she was to be struck with the greatest loss of them all – of her dear father, the light of her heart.

After the Prophet ﷺ had performed the Farewell Pilgrimage, he became seriously ill. Fatima went to visit him at Aisha's home ؑ. He welcomed her with a cheerful face and then whispered in her ear, and she wept intensely. Then he ﷺ whispered again in her ear and she laughed.

Aisha ؑ said, "I have never seen a day in which joy was as close to sorrow as I have seen today. I wanted to know the reason so I asked Fatima to tell me what made her cry and what made her smile. But she said, 'I could not reveal the secret of the Messenger of Allah.' "

During the death pangs of the Prophet ﷺ, she said, "What distress is afflicting my father!" The Prophet ﷺ said, "No distress will afflict your father anymore." When the Prophet ﷺ died, Fatima was grief-stricken and tears rolled down her bright cheeks. She kept repeating the words, "My father! My father! He answered the call of his Lord. Paradise is his abode. How close he is to his Lord!"

When the Prophet ﷺ was buried, she asked Anas, "O Anas, how could you willingly hurl earth over the Messenger of Allah ﷺ?" Then she wept, as did Ali and all the Muslims.

Afterwards, Aisha asked Fatima again, "Would you please tell me what the Prophet ﷺ whispered to you?" Fatima said,

> Now, I may. As for the first time he whispered to me, he ﷺ said, "Jibril used to review the Glorious Quran with me once a year, but this year, he reviewed it twice. Thus, I think that I am about to die. You should fear Allah and be patient. I am your best predecessor." Accordingly, I

wept. But when he noticed my sorrow, he whispered, "Fatima, would you like to be the mistress of the women in Paradise? You will be the first of my family to die after me." Then, I smiled.

Only months after the Prophet ﷺ had passed away, Fatima fell very ill, stricken by the grief of separation from her beloved father. One morning, early in the month of Ramadan, Fatima woke up with a look of happiness on her face. She called Salma bint Umays, who was looking after her, to prepare a bath. She then put on new clothes and perfumed herself and asked Salma to put her bed in the courtyard of the house. She then asked for her husband Ali, who was taken aback when he saw her lying with her face turned towards the sky. He asked her what was wrong, but she smiled and said, "I have an appointment today with the Messenger of God."

Ali wept at the side of his beloved wife as she tried to console him. She asked him to look after their children and advised that she should be buried without ceremony. She gazed upwards again, then closed her eyes and surrendered her soul.

Fatima al-Zahra had died soon after her father, thus fulfilling the Prophet's prophecy. She was only twenty-seven years old but had experienced so much in her lifetime. May Allah be pleased with the most cherished daughter of the Messenger of Allah ﷺ.

THE COMPANIONS

KHAWLA BINT HAKIM

Khawla, along with her husband, Uthman ibn Mazun, were among the first people to embrace Islam with every inch of their hearts. Khawla was a frequent visitor to Khadija's house and she greatly admired the noble lady, having sincere love for both her and her husband, the Messenger of Allah ﷺ.

After Khadija ؓ passed away, Khawla sensed the depth of the Prophet's loneliness and saw it shadow his noble face. Other women witnessed this sorrow too but Khawla was the only one who dared to address it. She said, "Messenger of Allah, it seems you have suffered much since the death of Khadija." The Prophet ﷺ replied, "Yes, she was the mother of the household and the caretaker for the family." Khawla wanted nothing more than to see the Prophet's heart find contentment and ease. With her maturity and farsightedness, she suggested that he marry again and suggested two potential brides who she deemed most worthy of him.

She gently introduced the notion into his head, saying "If you like, you can marry a mature woman or if you prefer you can marry a virgin, O Messenger of Allah." The Prophet ﷺ appreciated Khawla's thoughtfulness and asked who was the virgin and who the widow. She informed him that the widow was Sawda bint Zama, a pious woman in need of his protection, and the virgin was Aisha, daughter of Abu Bakr, who was the Prophet's most beloved friend.

Khawla's wisdom shone through in these two choices. Sawda who was an experienced woman who could take care of the Prophet's family and household, and Aisha was young woman who might mend his broken heart as well as strengthen the relationship between the Prophet ﷺ and his greatest support, Abu Bakr.

The Messenger of Allah ﷺ then told Khawla, "Mention me to them." So Khawla began her work as the go-between and matchmaker, bringing the happy news to Umm Romaan, Aisha's mother. Umm Romaan was overjoyed at the prospect of the blessed union. Khawla then went to Sawda to inform her that she was offered marriage by the best of creation. Khawla said, "Would you like Allah to give you great blessing, Sawda?" Sawda asked, "And what is that, Khawla?" She said, "The Messenger of Allah has sent me to you with a proposal of marriage!" Sawda was overjoyed and said, "I would like that! Please go to my father and tell him." Khawla went to Zama, an old man, greeted him and then said, "Muhammad son of Abdullah son of Abdul Muttalib has sent me to ask for Sawda in marriage." The old man exclaimed, "A noble match! What does she say?" Khawla replied, "She would like that." He told her to call Sawda to him. When she came, he said, "Sawda, this woman claims that Muhammad son of Abdullah son of Abdul Muttalib has sent her to ask for you in marriage. It is a noble match. Do you want me to marry you to him?" Sawda, with happiness in her heart, said that she accepted.

Khawla became friendly with all the Prophet's wives, who always welcomed her graciously into their homes. Once, they noticed that she looked very plain, caring little about how she dressed. They asked her the reason for her neglected appearance when her husband was so rich. Khawla replied, "He is in his own world, fasting every day and standing up in voluntary worship every night." They mentioned Khawla's situation to the Prophet ﷺ, who went to her husband saying, "Uthman, am I not the one you should follow?" Uthman wondered what the Prophet ﷺ was alluding to and when the Prophet ﷺ mentioned his night worship and fasting, Uthman confirmed that he did. The Prophet ﷺ said, "Do not do so. Your eyes have a claim on you, your body has a claim on you, your family has a claim on you. You may worship a little and go to sleep, and you may fast some days, but not every day." Uthman acted on the Prophet's advice and became more caring towards his wife, so that when Khawla next visited the Prophet's wives, she was well dressed, looking almost like a bride. Later, when Uthman was the first Muslim from Mecca to die in Medina, Khawla composed a poem highlighting his virtues.

Khawla was herself a deeply virtuous and selfless woman. It was through her diplomacy, maturity and foresight, that she successfully arranged the marriages between the noble Prophet ﷺ and Sawda and Aisha ؓ, the mothers of the believers. May Allah be pleased with Khawla bint Hakim, the blessed matchmaker.

ASMA BINT ABU BAKR

Asma bint Abu Bakr, Aisha's ؓ half-sister, was one of the first people to accept Islam at the age of seventeen. She was astute, dignified and generous, as well as courageous and resilient in the face of fear. Asma, who was many years older than Aisha, was like a mother to her.

As the daughter of the first man to enter Islam, Abu Bakr al-Siddiq, Asma saw the Prophet ﷺ come to her father's house every day to visit his closest friend. After witnessing thirteen years of pain and torture unleashed on the Prophet ﷺ, her father and the growing group of Muslims, Asma was about to be involved in a highly confidential incident.

Abu Bakr's son had found out the Quraysh's intention to kill the Prophet ﷺ and had stationed two young men at his door to watch him. Abu Bakr formulated a secret plan of escape, and Asma was one of a handful of individuals to know of it. The Prophet ﷺ had slipped out of his house to Abu Bakr's house, and together, from there, they were to head for the mountains and hide in the Cave of Thawr before continuing to Medina.

Asma carefully prepared days worth of food and water for the Prophet ﷺ and her father. But they needed to find a way to carry the provisions through the rocky and rugged mountainous paths. The quick-thinking Asma decided to use her waistband or *nitaaq*. Asma tore it into two and used one part to tie the food container and the other to tie the water skin. The Messenger of Allah ﷺ looked at her with a smile and said, "Indeed, Allah has given you, in exchange for this waistband, two waistbands in Paradise." From then on, Asma earned her nickname *dhat an-nitaaqayn*, the one with the two waistbands.

As soon as the Quraysh discovered that the Prophet ﷺ had fled, they were consumed with rage. The Prophet's bitterest enemy, Amr ibn Hisham, known as Abu Jahl, brewed in anger when he learned that the Prophet ﷺ had managed to escape and that he had left from Abu Bakr's house. He knocked violently at the door and Asma came out to meet him, maintaining her nerve. When he demanded to know where her father was, she courageously replied, "I do not know." Abu Jahl raised his hand and slapped her so hard on the face that her earrings were dislodged. He tried to force her to disclose their hiding place, but she bravely stood her ground until Abu Jahl finally gave up and left. Asma had protected her father and the Prophet ﷺ and they eventually reached safety in Medina.

Just before her own migration to Medina, Asma had married al-Zubayr ibn al-'Awwam. Al-Zubayr was poor, possessing little more than the horse he rode upon. She relates,

> Al-Zubayr married me while he owned nothing but his horse. I used to provide fodder for the horse, give it water and groom it. I would grind grain and make dough, but I could not bake well. The women of the Ansar used to bake for me. They were truly good women. I used to carry the grain on my head from al-Zubayr's plot, which the Prophet had allocated to him to cultivate. It was about three *farsakh* [about eight kilometres] from the town's centre. One day I was on the road carrying the grain on my head when I met the Prophet and a group of Companions. He called out to me and stopped his camel so that I could ride behind him. I felt embarrassed to travel with the Prophet and also remembered al-Zubayr's jealousy, he was the most jealous of men. The Prophet realised that I was embarrassed and rode on.

When Asma related to al-Zubayr what had happened, he said, "By Allah, that you should have to carry grain is far more distressing to me than your riding with [the Prophet]".

Asma was pregnant during the final emigration from Mecca to Medina. But nothing, neither the prospect of the arduous journey nor her pregnancy, deterred her from migrating. As soon as she reached Quba on the outskirts of Medina, she gave birth to a son, and they named him Abdullah. Abdullah was the first child to be born in Medina to the companions who migrated to Medina in Allah's cause, known as the Muhajirun. They celebrated, exclaiming, '*Allahu Akbar!* and '*Laa ilaaha illa Allah*' in joy and gratitude.

As he grew up, Abdullah witnessed and admired his mother's abundant generosity. He said,

I have not seen two women more generous than my aunt Aisha and my mother Asma. But their generosity was expressed in different ways. My aunt would accumulate one thing after another until she had gathered what she felt was sufficient and then distributed it all to those in need. My mother, on the other hand, would not keep anything even for the next day.

Asma was also a woman of keen intelligence. Her presence of mind in difficult circumstances, as she had shown when the Prophet ﷺ and Abu Bakr escaped, was remarkable. When her father left Mecca, he took all his wealth, amounting to some 6,000 dirhams. When Abu Bakr's blind father, Abu Quhafa, who was still a polytheist, heard of his departure, he told Asma, "I understand that he has left you bereft of money after he himself has abandoned you." Asma replied, "No, grandfather, in fact he has left us much money." She quickly gathered some pebbles and placed them in a small opening in the wall where they used to keep money and threw a cloth over the heap. She then took her grandfather's hand and said, "Feel how much money he has left us". She wanted to allay the fears of the old man and prevent him from giving her anything of his own wealth, as he was still not a Muslim.

Asma's mother, Qatayla, who had also refused to accept Islam, once came to Medina to visit her daughter bearing gifts of raisins, clarified butter and acacia pods. Asma, placing the love for her faith above her love for her mother, at first refused to receive her or to accept her gifts. She wanted to find out if she was permitted to allow her non-Muslim mother into her home, so she sent someone to the Prophet ﷺ asking if she should keep good ties with her?" The Prophet ﷺ replied, "Yes, keep good ties with your mother" (Bukhari and Muslim).

A few years after the Prophet's death, Asma showed the steel of her courage on the battlefield. She was instrumental at the Battle of Yarmouk in 636, a major battle between the Byzantines and the Muslim forces which marked the first great wave of early Muslim conquests. The Muslims were hugely outnumbered by the Romans, but with the help of the women among them, they drove the Roman Empire out of Syria. The early Muslim historian and biographer of the Prophet ﷺ, al-Waqidi, who specialised in his military campaigns, wrote that the women fought harder than the men. Asma also knew how to defend herself away from battle. She kept a dagger to defend herself when thieves appeared in Medina at the time of Said ibn al-Aas, the Muslim governor of Kufa under Caliph Uthman.

Armed with such fighting spirit, it's no wonder that Asma lived until she was 100 years old. She was frail and lost her sight, but even towards the end of her life, she showed strength of mind and took a significant stand against al-Hajjaj ibn Yusuf, the ruthless and harsh leader who had defeated her son, Abdullah, in battle. Finding his army crushed, Abdullah rushed to his mother's side, seeking her advice on al-Hajjaj's siege on Mecca. Abdullah addressed her saying,

> The people have deserted me out of fear of al-Hajjaj or being tempted by what he has to offer. Even my children and my family have left me. There is only a small group of men with me now and however strong and steadfast they are, they can only resist for an hour or two more. Messengers of the Banu Umayya [the Umayyads] are now negotiating with me, offering to give me whatever worldly possessions I want. Should I lay down my arms and swear allegiance to Abdul Malik ibn Marwan? What do you think?

Raising her voice, she replied,

> It's your affair Abdullah, and you know yourself better. If, however, you think that you are right and that you are standing up for the Truth, then persevere and fight on as your companions who were killed under your flag had shown perseverance. If, however, you desire the world, what a miserable wretch you are. You would have destroyed yourself and you would have destroyed your men.

He replied, "But I will be killed today, there is no doubt about it." Asmaa responded, "That is better for you than that you should surrender yourself to Hajjaj voluntarily and that some minions of Banu Umayyah should play with your head." Abdullah proclaimed, "I do not fear death. I am only afraid that they will mutilate me." Asmaa assured him, "There is nothing after death that man should be afraid of. Skinning does not cause any pain to the slaughtered sheep." Abdullah exclaimed,

What a blessed mother! Blessed be your noble qualities! I have come to you at this hour to hear what I have heard. God knows that I have not weakened or despaired. He is witness over me that I have not stood up for what I have out of love for this world and its attractions but only out of anger for the sake of God. His limits have been transgressed. Here am I, going to what is pleasing to you. So if I am killed, do not grieve for me and commend me to God.

Asma resolutely replied, "I shall grieve for you only if you are killed in a vain and an unjust cause."

She approached Abdullah to embrace him and found that he was wearing an armour plate. She said, "This, my son, is not the dress of one who desires martyrdom. Take it off. That will make your movements lighter and quicker." Abdullah removed his armour and went back to fight. He did not stop fighting until he was killed. Al-Hajjaj issued a command to have him crucified. Ibn al-Sakan reported on the authority of Yahya al-Taymi, from his father, that he said,

I entered Mecca after Ibn al-Zubayr was killed and I saw him crucified. I saw his mother Asma who was a tall, blind old woman. She went to Hajjaj and stood before him. He approached and said, "O Mother, the Commander of the Faithful Abd al-Malik Ibn Marwan has recommended me to treat you well. Do you need anything?" She shouted, "I am not your mother. I am the mother of that one crucified on the cross. I don't need you. Is it not time for this rider to dismount?" Hajjaj responded, "He is a hypocrite!" But his mother retorted, "No, he was never a hypocrite. He was rather a constant performer of voluntary fasting and prayer." Hajjaj then said, "Go away, you old and senile woman." She again retorted, "I am not senile. I have heard the Messenger of Allah saying that there would come out of the tribe of Thaqifa a liar and a ruthless murderer. As for the liar, we have already seen him, as for the ruthless murderer, it is you."

In another version, when al-Hajjaj came to Asma ؓ he said, "How did I punish your son, Asma?" She replied quietly, "You spoiled his life, but he spoiled your next life." Al-Hajjaj could not compete with Asma's resolute determination. He had no other choice than to bring the corpse of Abdullah ibn al-Zubayr down from the cross.

Asma was not destined to live for many more days after Abdullah's death. Having lived a long life of struggle, perseverance and courage against every trial, Asma ﷺ surrendered her soul only ten days after her son had fallen in battle. May Allah be pleased with the lady of the two waistbands.

FATIMA BINT AL-KHATTAB

Fatima bint al-Khattab ibn Nufayl ibn Abdul Uzza, was a woman who helped transformed an enemy of Islam into its greatest champion. Fatima bint al-Khattab was sister to the mighty Umar, a future caliph of the Muslims, but who had bitterly opposed the Prophet ﷺ before he became a Muslim.

Despite the threat of her brother's anger, Fatima bint al-Khattab showed incredible courage and conviction in embracing Islam. She belonged to the house of al-Khattab ibn Nufayl al-Makhzumi, one of the noblest and most elite houses of the Quraysh.

Fatima bint al-Khattab ﷺ married the sincere and gracious Said ibn Zayd, who embraced Islam at the hands of the honourable companion, Khabab ibn al-Arat. Khabab took Said to the Prophet ﷺ to declare his faith. Said then went back to his wife and told her about the new faith and she was so impressed with the beauties of its teachings, that no sooner did he finish his speech than she embraced Islam as well.

Khabbab visited the pure hearted couple often, finding them eager students of the Glorious Quran and the tenets of Islam. Knowing the opposition of their families, Fatima and her husband concealed their belief so they could escape the persecution dealt out by their families. Especially Fatima's brother, Umar, who wanted to eradicate Islam and kill the Prophet ﷺ.

One day, Umar was menacingly gripping a sword in his hand and made his way towards Dar al-Arqam, the safe house where the Prophet ﷺ taught his companions about Islam. Someone asked him, "Where are you going, Umar? Why are you carrying your sword?" Umar replied, "I am going to kill Muhammad, who has divided us and insulted our gods." The man said, "Do you think that Banu Abd Manaf would allow you to do that without taking vengeance?" The man then suggested that instead of killing Muhammad, it would be better to look to his own household. Umar was shocked and enraged and demanded, "What do you mean and whom do you mean?" The man answered, "Your sister, Fatima, and your brother-in-law, Said ibn Zayd. They have followed Muhammad!" Umar then said, "Are you sure? Woe unto them from me!"

Burning with rage, Umar turned in the direction of their house, with the intention of killing them for their betrayal. When he arrived at their house, he heard them reciting words he did not understand. He angrily beat his fist on the door, calling loudly upon his sister. Khabab, who was teaching them, hid himself in a corner of the house to ensure their secret would not be found out, while Fatima concealed the copy from which they read. Umar charged in and asked, "What was the murmuring I heard?" "It was nothing," they replied. Umar was implacable. He told them he heard that they follow Muhammad and that if that were true there would be severe consequences.

It was at this moment that Fatima's courage rose up to meet her brother's anger. She confronted him boldly and declared, without an ounce of fear, that she and her husband had accepted Islam and testified that there is no deity worthy of being worshipped but Allah and that Muhammad is the Messenger of Allah. Umar could no longer contain his rage. He pounced on Said and threw him to the floor. When Fatima dashed forward to defend her husband, Umar gave her a brutal slap on her face, and she started bleeding.

Umar saw the blood flowing from his sister's face and suddenly felt remorse in his heart. He moved to Said, lifted him from the floor and turned to his sister, Fatima, to wipe the blood from her face. Umar was so struck with their sincerity and fortitude that he asked to see the leaf from which they had been reading. Fatima said, "You are impure. You must first purify yourself." Umar performed his ablution, the water calming his anger, and he began to read the revealed words of God. They touched his soul. The leaf contained a portion of Surah Taha, and Umar read up to the words, "The Hour is coming – though I choose to keep it hidden – for each soul to be rewarded for its labour" (Quran 20:15).

Umar said, "What honourable words!" Upon hearing Umar's comment, Khabbab ibn al-Arat came out of his hiding place saying, "O Umar, I hope that the Prophet's supplication be answered. He invoked

Allah saying, 'O Allah! May you support Islam with the closest one to you – either Abu Jahl ibn Hisham or Umar ibn al-Khattab.' The latter was the closest one."

Umar went to the Prophet ﷺ to profess his faith before him and to join the Muslim community. Having the mighty Umar on their side was a victory for the Muslims. With Umar's acceptance of Islam, the call of Islam emerged out of secrecy and into the open, and Fatima bint al-Khattab had been the key.

Because of her courage and bold faith, she had transformed the wrath of her brother into love and vital support for the Prophet ﷺ and his mission. Fatima bint al-Khattab's name can be remembered in the turning point for early Islam, may Allah be pleased with her.

UMM KULTHUM BINT ALI IBN ABU TALIB

Umm Kulthum was born into the noblest of lineages. She was the cherished granddaughter of the Prophet Muhammad ﷺ and the daughter of Fatima and Ali – cousin to the Prophet ﷺ and one of the Rightly Guided Caliphs. Umm Kulthum grew up alongside her sister, Zaynab, and brothers Hasan and Husayn, in a household filled with blessing. She grew into a paragon of piety and goodness.

Umar ibn al-Khattab, who was the leader of the believers at that time, asked for her hand in marriage, but Ali refused him because she was young and because he intended for her to marry her cousin, Awn son of Jafar. However, Umar's heart was set on her and he wished for nothing more honourable than being joined to a member of the Prophet's household. He pleaded, "Give her to me in marriage, Abu al-Hassan, because I will be devoted to her, and no other man will care for her like I will."

Ali said, "I will send her to you, if you like her, I shall marry her to you." Ali then sent Umm Kulthum with a garment and told her to say to Umar, "This is the cloth that I was talking about". When Umar received her and heard what she said, he told her, "Tell your father that I am pleased, I am pleased, I am pleased, may Allah be pleased with you." When she returned to her father, Ali asked her what Umar had said, and she informed him of his words. Ali was satisfied and decided to give Umar her hand in marriage.

Thus, Umar, the second caliph of Islam, married the Prophet's granddaughter in the month of Dhul Qadah, 17 AH.

Umm Kulthum and Umar were blessed with two children, Zayd ibn Umar and Ruqayya bint Umar. There is a beautiful account of Umm Kulthum and Umar, which demonstrates their humble nature and their desire to serve others. Once, Umar went out as usual to check on the welfare of the people when he heard a woman's cry coming from a hut. A man was standing at the door, so Umar greeted him and asked where he came from. The man said that he was a Bedouin and that he had come to find the leader of the believers, hoping to receive some of his generosity. The Bedouin did not know that he was addressing the caliph himself. Umar asked him who had let out the cry he heard. "It is my wife giving birth," the man replied, "and there is no one to help her." Umar rushed back home to Umm Kulthum asking her, "Would you like to gain a reward from Allah?" She said, "What form of goodness and reward is it, O Umar? " As soon as Umar explained, Umm Kulthum hastily made preparations and set out to the hut to assist the mother in the pangs of her labour. Umar went with Umm Kulthum, carrying a pot full of oil and grains.

Umm Kulthum went inside the hut and took on the role of the midwife. Umar, the leader of the believers, sat down outside with the Bedouin and began to cook. When the Bedouin's wife gave birth, Umm Kulthum called out to her husband, "O Leader of the Believers, tell your companion that Allah has blessed him with a son." The Bedouin was speechless to hear that the man who had been cooking for him and his wife was none other than the Caliph of Islam. The woman who had just given birth was also surprised to discover that her midwife was the wife of the Leader of the Believers. Together, Umar and Umm Kulthum demonstrated how they served the people, with the utmost humility and courtesy.

After many years of expanding the Muslim empire, Umar was killed by a Persian slave, leaving Umm Kulthum a widow. Umm Kulthum then married her young cousin, Awn, for a dowry of 4,000 dirhams. She loved him greatly, but he died shortly into their marriage.

Ali then married her to Awn's brother, who also passed away. She then married a third brother.

Umm Kulthum passed away in 75 AH. It's said that when she died, her son Zayd died on the same day and they were carried together on the funeral bier. She was buried in Damascus in Syria, may Allah be pleased with Umm Kulthum, granddaughter of the Prophet ﷺ.

SAFIYA BINT ABDUL MUTTALIB

Safiya bint Abdul Muttalib was the Prophet's aunt and sister to the 'Lion of Allah', Hamza ibn Abdul Muttalib. Like her brother, Safiya was fierce, strong and brave. She was also highly eloquent and intelligent. She ﷺ was brought up in a noble house, and her family was responsible for providing water to the pilgrims visiting the Holy Kaaba.

Her first marriage was to al-Harith ibn Umayyah, Abu Sufyan's brother, yet he died before they had any children together. She was then married to al-Awwam ibn Khuwaylid, Lady Khadja's ﷺ brother.

They had two children, al-Sa'ib and al-Zubayr. When al-Awwam passed away, Safiya devoted all her attention to her two orphaned sons, especially the younger son, Zubayr. It was her intention to make him strong and resilient so that he could survive through life. Whenever he came home complaining of being bullied by children of his age, she would rebuke him, hit him and toughen him up herself.

Safiya was among the first to enter Islam, yet her son Zubayr embraced Islam before his mother. She argued with him when he became Muslim, but he was an independent, strong man, just as his mother had brought him up to be. Despite her stern opposition, he still treated his mother with honour and compassion. But when the day came that her own brother, Hamza, chose Islam, Safiya was ready to answer its call as well.

Safiya became an asset to the early Muslims. She joined the Muslim army at Uhud in 625 to treat the wounded and serve the warriors. When the Muslims started to withdraw from the battlefield, she advanced and urged them to go back and defend their faith. She waved an arrow in their faces, saying, "Would you leave the Prophet ﷺ alone?" Hammad narrated on the authority of Hisham that 'Urwah said, "Safiya came on the day of Uhud while the Muslims were vanquished, holding a spear in her hand and striking the faces of the polytheists with it. When the Messenger of Allah ﷺ saw her, he called her son to take hold of her lest she be harmed, for she was his [the Prophet's] aunt."

When Safiya heard that her brother Hamza, whom she dearly loved, had been martyred, she made her way through the battlefield to see him.

Hamza had been mutilated by the enemy; his belly pierced open, his nose cut off and his ears severed. Before she reached her brother's body, her son, Zubayr, stood in her way out of concern and told her, "My mother, Allah's Messenger is ordering you to go back!" But the persevering woman told her son Zubayr, "Why should I go back since I have heard that my brother was mutilated in the cause of Allah? We are not pleased with what has happened, but I will bear it with patience, and I hope to get the reward from Allah, if He so Wills." Zubayr came back to the Messenger of Allah ﷺ and informed him of what she had said. The Prophet ﷺ then said, "Let her go [to see her brother]." She then went to Hamza ﷺ and stood beside his corpse. She shed tears, sought Allah's forgiveness and said, "*Inna lillahi wa inna ilahi raji'un* [Certainly we belong to Allah and to Him we are to return]."

Two years later, Safiya proved her fearless heroism again. This time it was at the Battle of the Trench, a thirty-day siege to defend Medina against the Quraysh and Jewish tribes who waged war against the Prophet ﷺ. When a Jewish spy attempted to attack the women's camp, the Muslim women and children took shelter in a fort guarded by Hassan ibn Thabit, who did not wish to go out and fight. Safiya saw a Jewish man moving around the fort, and she went to Hasan saying, "I am suspicious of that man, since he might lead the enemy to us. You have to kill him." Hassan replied, "May Allah forgive you, I cannot do that."

Safiya decided to take the matter into her own hands. She veiled herself, picked up a huge cudgel and went down to the fort. She stealthily came up behind him and hit him on the back of his head several times until he died. She had managed to protect the fort of Muslim women by killing the spy.

When the Prophet ﷺ died, Safiya spoke words of eulogy. Ibn Ishaq reported some lines of the poem, which reads as follows, "The day we miss the Messenger of Allah is here! O eyes! Shed abundant and plentiful tears!" She was also reported to have also said, "The day of your death is certainly a day in which the sun is wrapped up in darkness though it is shining!"

Safiya led a life of sacrifice and bravery until she died during the era of Umar ibn al-Khattab, when she was about seventy years old. May Allah be pleased with Safiya bint Abdul Muttalib, the Prophet's aunt.

SUMAYA BINT KHAYYAT

Sumaya bint Khayyat ؓ was the seventh person to enter Islam, and she was the first woman to sacrifice her life for it. Sumaya was the servant of Abu Hudhayfa ibn al-Mughira and was given in marriage by her master to a Yemeni emigrant, Yasir.

Sumaya and Yasir soon had two children, Ammar and Ubaydulla. Ammar heard about the new faith and, after a long period of meditation, he embraced Islam. He went home to tell his parents what the Prophet ﷺ was preaching. Convinced by the truth of what they heard, Sumaya and Yasir embraced Islam without hesitation. Strengthened in heart by their new faith, Sumaya, Yasir and Ammar did not keep their belief a secret. One of the wealthiest tribes of Quraysh, Banu Makhzum, began their campaign of persecution and targeted the poorer and weaker in status among them, hoping that through fear they would turn their backs on Islam.

The Quraysh began to inflict their cruelty on Sumaya, Yasir and Ammar, taking them into the burning desert of Mecca where they suffered severe torture. They were forced to stand in the scorching sun dressed in mail-coats, the heat piercing their bodies like arrows of fire. They were also lashed with swords and spears, but Sumaya, her husband and son refused to give up their faith. The Messenger of Allah ﷺ used to go to their place of persecution and have tears in his eyes for their suffering. He honoured them for their fortitude and heroism, saying, "Keep patient, the household of Yasir. For truly, Paradise will be your meeting place." The Prophet's ﷺ words brought relief and peace to their hearts, and they forgot their pain. Sumaya proudly recited, "I testify that you are the Messenger of Allah and that your promise is truthful." She had no fear of death, she knew it was in Allah's cause.

Abu Jahl passed by to insult and rebuke them. Sumaya's reply was a spit in his face. Incensed, Abu Jahl mercilessly struck a spear into her private parts. Safiya fell to the ground and died as Islam's first martyr. She had endured the worst forms of torture yet never gave up her faith and died a true warrior of Islam. God brought her justice when Abu Jahl was later killed at the Battle of Badr, and Muhammad ﷺ said to Ammar, "Allah has killed your mother's killer."

May Allah have mercy on Sumaya bint Khayyat, an enduring symbol of sacrifice and steadfast faith, and Islam's first martyr.

ASMA BINT YAZID

Asma bint Yazid ibn al-Sakan, was a distinguished figure among the women of the Ansar. She was rational and religious and was called "the orator of women" because of her eloquence of speech. Asma belonged to the clan of Abd al-Ashhal of the Aws, whose chief was Saad ibn Mu'adh. She and Kabshah bint Rafi, Saad's own mother, were the first women of the Ansar to pledge their loyalty to the Prophet ﷺ after he arrived in Medina.

Such a pledge was mentioned in the glorious Quran. Allah the Almighty says,

> Prophet, when believing women come and pledge to you that they will not ascribe any partner to God, nor steal, nor commit adultery, nor kill their children, nor lie about who has fathered their children, nor disobey you in any righteous thing, then you should accept their pledge of allegiance and pray to God to forgive them. God is most forgiving and merciful. (Quran 60:12)

Having given the pledge, Asma bint Yazid ﷺ was curious to know everything about Islam. Due to her thirst for knowledge, Asma was a regular student of the Prophet's gatherings. She is the most distinguished reporter of the Prophet's hadiths from among the Ansari women, reporting no less than eighty-one hadiths. In one report, she speaks of the revelation of Surah al-Ma'idah (Chapter of The Feast). She reports, "I was holding the rein of al-Adbaa, the Prophet's she-camel, when Surah al-Ma'idah was revealed to him in full. It was so heavy, that it almost broke the limbs of the she-camel."

Asma bint Yazid was regarded as the representative of the Ansari women and never shied of asking questions that would benefit them, and it was she who asked the Prophet ﷺ about the rulings of menstruation. She once approached the Prophet ﷺ when he was sitting with a group of his male companions and said,

> Messenger of God ﷺ, I am sent by a group of Muslim women and we all share the same view and have the same concern. Allah has sent you to both men and women. We believe in you and follow you. Yet we, women, have to stay at home. We are the object of men's desire and

we bear their children. Nevertheless, men have privileges, such as the obligatory Friday prayer, attending funerals and going on *jihad* campaigns. When they leave for *jihad*, we look after their property and we rear their children. Messenger of God ﷺ, do we have a share of reward for doing so?

The Prophet ﷺ turned to the men attending him and said, "Have you ever heard a more eloquent woman putting a case concerning her faith?" They said, "We never thought that a woman can be so expressive". The Prophet ﷺ said to her, "Asma, go and tell women that when any of you is a goodly wife, giving her husband a pleasant life and cutting out friction, she earns a reward equal to all that you have mentioned of men's reward".

Asma ؓ belonged to a family of brave fighters. In the Battle of Uhud, when the Muslim army was in disarray, her brother, Imara ibn Yazid ؓ, was one of the few who remained to defend the Prophet ﷺ to the death. Her father and uncle were also killed in the same battle. The courageous Asma, like her family members, was also eager to go out on the battlefield for Allah's cause. She accompanied the Prophet ﷺ on his expedition that led to the fall of Mecca to Islam.

A few years after the Prophet's ﷺ death, Asma joined the Muslim forces to face the Byzantine army at the battle of Yarmouk. She took part in the fighting, using the pole of her own tent to defend herself and the women with her, killing nine Roman soldiers. She was also among the women who stood behind the ranks of the Muslim warriors, blocking the way of those trying to flee the battlefield and encouraging them to return. She also provided the warriors with food and water and treated the wounded.

After the victory of battle, when Syria came under Muslim rule, Asma stayed in Damascus, teaching women about Islam. Having lived a life of heroism and knowledge, Asma died in 30 AH at around the age of ninety and is buried in Damascus. May Allah be pleased with Asma bint Yazid, an orator, a student and a warrior.

UMM SULAYM BINT MALHAN

Umm Sulaym bint Malhan, also nicknamed Rumaysa, was known for her excellent character and the power of her intellect, as well as a strong independence of mind. She was an Ansari woman and one of the earliest Muslims in Medina to embrace Islam. She was influenced by the eloquent and persuasive Musab ibn Umayr, who was sent as Islam's first emissary by the Prophet ﷺ. Umm Sulaym was also the Prophet's aunt from his maternal side, either by suckling or by blood.

Umm Sulaym became Muslim while she was married to her cousin, Malik ibn al-Nadr, who rejected Islam and tried his best to make her forsake her new faith. But she had already begun to instruct their son, Anas ibn Malik, who was to be one of the Prophet's closest companions and a major narrator of Hadith. Umm Sulaym taught Anas to testify that "there is no god but Allah and Muhammad is the Messenger of Allah." Anas repeated what his mother said, but his polytheist father said to his wife, "Do not corrupt my child." She replied, "I am not corrupting him. I want to educate him." Malik was furious. He decided to leave his home forever unless she converted. But Umm Sulaym would never give up her faith. No sooner did he leave the house than he was killed at the hands of one of his enemies.

Umm Sulaym found out what had happened to her husband and was shocked, but she was not gravely upset by the news. She knew she could now freely devote herself to Islam and to bring up her son in its fold. Later on, Umm Sulaym thought the best place for Anas would be by the side of the Prophet ﷺ himself, so she offered her son to him as a servant and was pleased when the Prophet ﷺ agreed and accepted.

When it was known that Umm Sulaym was a widow, Zayd ibn Sahl, known as Abu Talha, resolved to make her a proposal. He was a wealthy man, a skilful archer and an accomplished horseman, so he was confident Umm Sulaym would accept him. Moreover, he was from the same clan as her, the Banu al-Najjar. However, he was still a pagan. Abu Talha offered her a precious gift as a dowry, expecting her to accept, but a challenge came back to him instead. Umm Sulaym knew that he had a wooden idol at home, which he venerated, and she prompted him to reflect on his ancestral beliefs. She said, "Abu Talha, don't you know that the deity that you worship grew from the earth?" He answered in the affirmative. She said, "Are you then not ashamed of worshipping a tree. While you use the rest of it to bake bread and keep yourself warm?" Her words began to enter his heart. Then Umm Sulaym added, "No one can reject the likes of you, Abu Talha. But you are a polytheist and I am a

Muslim. I am not allowed to marry a polytheist. My dowry is for you to embrace Islam. Nothing else" (Nasai).

Abu Talha was greatly impressed with Umm Sulaym and went away to reflect deeply on what she said. He came back after a while and said, "I testify that there is no deity worthy of worship except Allah and I testify that Muhammad is the Messenger of Allah!" As soon as he became a Muslim, Umm Sulaym married him. She became the first Muslim woman to accept Islam as her dowry.

Having embraced Islam, Abu Talha's soul was touched with the majesty of his new faith and he put all his energies into serving it. He swore allegiance to the Prophet ﷺ at the second pledge of Aqaba – one report says Umm Sulaym was present with him. Abu Talha had a beautiful orchard called Bayraha which was bursting with date palms, grapes and running water. Abu Talha valued it greatly, and he went to the Prophet ﷺ and said, "What I love most is Bayraha. Therefore, I give it in charity for the sake of Allah. I want Allah's reward. Thus, you may place it wherever you want, Messenger of Allah." The Prophet ﷺ was moved by his generosity but said to Abu Talha, "Oh no! That is a blessed property. I think it is better to consecrate it for your kin." And Abu Talha distributed it among his Muslim relatives. (Bukhari)

Allah blessed Umm Sulaym and Abu Talha with a son, whom they called Abu Umayr. The child brought the couple so much happiness, but their joy was to be darkened with tragedy. Their little boy fell ill and it was Allah's will to test the new parents by taking their child's soul back to Him. Abu Talha was away from home and did not know about the death of his son. Umm Sulam peacefully covered the child, saying, "To Allah we are destined to return." She asked her family not to tell Abu Talha what had happened to the child as she wanted to find the easiest way for him to bear the news, knowing he would be utterly devastated.

When Abu Talha returned, he asked her about the child and she said, "He is very quiet." Then she brought her husband a meal, put on a beautiful dress, adorned herself and applyed perfume. She was so charming that he made love to her. In the morning, Umm Sulaym said to her husband, "What would you say if someone lent someone something. Could he refuse to give it back?" He replied, "No." She said, "Our son was just a trust from Allah, and He restored him to Himself." Abu Talha could hardly believe his ears. He said, "Why didn't you tell me before I indulged in such impurity?" But she kept appeasing him until he said, "To Allah we are destined to return."

In the morning, he went to the Prophet ﷺ with sorrow in his eyes, complaining of his wife's conduct. The Prophet ﷺ said, "May Allah bless your night." The Prophet's supplication was answered in the best possible way, for it led to a blessing that extended through generations. Umm Sulaym had become pregnant. When she gave birth, she sent the baby boy to the Prophet ﷺ who chewed a date and then rubbed the child's mouth with it. The Prophet ﷺ called him Abdullah (Bukhari and Muslim). Abdullah was later blessed with many children, ten of whom memorised the Quran completely.

Umm Sulaym and Abu Talha's complete selflessness is seen in a story about their hosting a poor man. Once this man came to the Prophet ﷺ and the Prophet ﷺ asked his wives if they had anything with which to feed the guest. But they all replied, "By He who sent you with the truth, we do not have anything but water." Then the Prophet ﷺ openly said, "May Allah have mercy on you, who can host him?" Then Abu Talha said, "I can, Messenger of Allah." Abu Talha brought the man home and asked Umm Sulaym, "Do we have anything to feed him?" She replied, "Nothing, other than the children's food." He said, "Put them to sleep and then pretend you are eating before the guest. When the guest begins to eat, pretend that you are repairing the lantern and then put it out." Under the cover of darkness, Umm Sulaym and her husband pretended they ate along with their guest but let him take his fill. Out of their sheer generosity and compassion for the poor man, they spent the night hungry, yet they earned Allah's pleasure. In the morning, Abu Talha went to the Prophet ﷺ. The Prophet ﷺ said to him, "Allah admired what you did with your guest last night." Allah the Exalted had revealed these verses to the Prophet ﷺ,

> Those who were already firmly established in their homes [in Medina] and firmly rooted in faith, show love for those who migrated to them for refuge and harbour no desire in their hearts for what has been given to them. They give them preference over themselves, even if they too are poor. Those who are saved from their own souls' greed are truly successful. (Quran 59:9)

Umm Sulaym and Abu Talha's home was one of the only homes the Prophet ﷺ visited. She held a special place in her heart for him, and she would be greatly honoured by his visits. He ﷺ would sometimes pray on the mat she provided, receive her refreshments if he were not fasting and take a siesta in her home. While he was sleeping, Umm Sulaym would gently collect the beads of perspiration that gathered on his brow. Once, the Prophet ﷺ woke from his slumber and asked, "Umm Sulaym, what are you doing?" She replied with the greatest love and respect, "O Prophet of Allah ﷺ, we seek blessings from it for our children." He ﷺ said, "What you are doing is right." (Sahih Muslim). Aisha bint Abi Bakr ؓ stated, "The sweat of the Holy Prophet ﷺ would seem like lustrous pearls on his face and its fragrance would be better than musk" (Subul ul-Huda War-Rashad). The Prophet ﷺ also showed Umm Sulaym deep love and respect and stated she would be among the dwellers of Paradise. The Prophet ﷺ said, "I entered Paradise, and I heard a rustle. I asked, 'Who is that?' They replied, 'That is al-Rumaysa bint Malhan, the mother of Anas ibn Malik.'" (Bukhari and Muslim).

Umm Sulaym never wished to be far from the Prophet ﷺ, even when it was at the time of battle. She went out with the Prophet ﷺ to serve in many conflicts where she lifted the spirit of the warriors, carried water for them and treated the wounded. She was also a brave warrior herself and she, like many other Muslim women, joined the Muslim soldiers to defend Islam. Umm Sulaym is most well known for her role in the battle of Hunayn, where she carried a dagger folded into her dress, even while she was pregnant. When Abu Talha saw her, he told the Prophet ﷺ, "O Messenger of Allah, Umm Sulaym has a dagger!" She said, "O Messenger of Allah, this is to defend myself, and if a polytheist approaches me, I will tear open his belly with it." The Prophet ﷺ commended her courage and she, in turn, defended the Prophet ﷺ in battle, spurred on by her love for the Messenger ﷺ and Allah.

Umm Sulaym bint Malhan ؓ was an extraordinary woman of deep-rooted faith, who was blessed with the Prophet's favour, a favour she deserved for her sacrifice and her unwavering loyalty to Islam. May Allah be pleased with the aunt of Prophet Muhammad ﷺ.

UMM HARAM BINT MALHAN

Umm Haram bint Malhan ibn Khalid was from among the Ansar and was one of the most pious and devoted women in Medina. Her family home was in Quba, which sat among date trees, springs and warm breezes. Umm Haram's home was one of the most beloved to the Prophet ﷺ. She was the sister of Umm Sulaym and an aunt of the Prophet ﷺ from his mother's side. Umm Haram has the status of being the first Muslim to die on a naval expedition.

Her nephew, Anas ibn Malik ﷺ, reported that the Prophet ﷺ used to visit Umm Haram as often as he could, and she was always eager to shower him with hospitality and kindness. She offered him ﷺ his favourite food, and when he finished eating, she would affectionately riffle his hair. One time, the Prophet ﷺ was sleeping in Umm Haram's house, when he woke up smiling. Umm Haram asked, "Why do you smile, Messenger of Allah?" He said, "I saw some people of my *ummah* on board a ship in the middle of the sea conquering in the cause of Allah. They were like kings on thrones." She said, "O Messenger of Allah, ask Allah to let me join them." He said, "You will be among the first of them."

Many years passed, during which the Prophet ﷺ died. All the while, Umm Haram did not forget his words, and yearned to travel the world by ship so that the word of Allah could spread far and wide. Her husband, Ubaada ibn al-Samit, was a commander in the Muslim army and was sent into Egypt under Umar's caliphate. Umm Haram accompanied her husband to the battle, and soon after the Muslim armies gained victory against the Romans, Umm Haram and Ubaada went to live in Damascus. Muawiya ibn Abi Sufiyan ﷺ was its governor at the time and feared for the city's harbours, which were being intermittently attacked by the Roman army. The Romans used Cyprus to station their ships, so he sent a message to Umar asking his permission to invade Cyprus. But Umar refused as he did not wish to put the lives of Muslims in danger. Later, when Uthman was Caliph, Muawiya renewed his request and was finally granted it. He began to call the Muslims to fight in Allah's cause. Umm Haram, along with her husband, set sail for Cyprus. Her heart was full of excitement and a fervent desire to please her Lord. She knew that the Prophet's ﷺ *dua* for her was finally being answered.

As the ship ploughed through the sea, she kept saying to herself,

"You said the truth, O Messenger of Allah!" When they arrived on the Cyprus coastline, the soldiers surged out preparing themselves for battle. But disembarking from the ship, Umm Haram's horse reared violently, and she was thrown from it and died. She was buried where she fell, in the island of Cyprus. May Allah be pleased with Umm Haram bint Malhan, the first naval martyr of Islam.

UMM WARAQA

Umm Waraqa was a dedicated Muslim, a memoriser of the Quran and a leader of prayer. She held a high and noble lineage and was the daughter of Abdullah ibn al-Harith. She was a wealthy member of the Ansar, yet she desired nothing but to die in Allah's cause.

In the Battle of Badr, Umm Waraqa asked the Prophet's ﷺ permission to join the Muslim army in order to treat the wounded. She said, "O Messenger of Allah, allow me to go out with you so that I could nurse the wounded among your Companions, and perhaps, Allah will bless me with martyrdom." The Prophet ﷺ said to her, "Stay home. Allah will grant you martyrdom." From that day onward, she was given the prestigious title of "the martyr".

Umm Waraqa entirely devoted herself to Islam and the Qur'an, which she recited with the deepest of humility. The Quran became her main concern and all aspects of her private and public life revolved around it. With each passing day, her *iman* grew stronger, and she drew closer and closer to Allah through fasting, prayer and recitation.

One day, she came to the Prophet ﷺ seeking permission to have a *muezzin* in her house, as the number of people living there were so numerous. He granted her request and commanded that Umm Waraqa lead the prayer. Umm Waraqa was overjoyed to be the *imama* of the people of her household, *ahl-ul dariha*. The most accepted opinion is that the people of Umm Waraqa's household were considered to be the women of her house – her female relatives, friends and servants. Yet the word '*dar*' holds ambiguity and can be translated not only as 'house', but also 'residence', 'area' or 'neighbourhood', which has opened an interpretation that the assembly may have included men. However, the scholars agree that it was a women-only congregation. Further, there are two potentially weak narrators in the chain of this hadith, which makes it questionable to use the tradition of Umm Waraqa as the basis for establishing any rulings in regard to a female *imam* leading a mixed congregation.

At any rate, Umm Waraqa was nothing less than an *imama* and dedicated Muslim. She continued to worship Allah fervently throughout her life until she reached old age. She did not marry and had no children, yet she had a housemaid and a male servant whom she treated like a loving mother. Umm Waraqa made a will that if she died, her female and male servant should be set free. It was at their hands that Umm Waraqa received the martyrdom she desired. They strangled her to death, impatient for the death of their mistress that would bring about their freedom. In the morning, Umar ibn al-Khattab said, "By Allah, I did not hear the recitation of Umm Waraqa last night." He checked her home and found her dead body wrapped in cloth. He said, "The Messenger of Allah was truthful when he used to say, 'let us go to visit the martyr'." Umar ordered the killers to be brought before him. They confessed to her murder, and their crime was met with justice. (ibn Hajar and al-Hakim)

May Allah have mercy on Umm Waraqa, who gained the martyrdom she was seeking.

ASMA BINT UMAYS

Asma bint Umays ibn Maad ibn Tamim, also called Umm Abdullah, had embraced Islam even before the Muslims began to gather at Dar al-Arqam. She was the wife of Jafar ibn Abu Talib, an honourable Companion and a cousin to the Prophet.

Asma and Jafar were newly married when they joined the early emigrants on the arduous journey to Abyssinia. They lived there for fifteen years, and Asma gave birth to three children, Abdullah, Muhammad and Awn. Abdullah looked like his father, Jafar, who resembled his cousin, the Messenger of Allah. Asma patiently waited throughout the years, yearning to rejoin the Muslim community. When news of the Prophet's command for the emigrants to go to Medina finally came through, she joined the caravan, filled with joy and hope.

No sooner did the delegation arrive at Medina than it was proclaimed that the Muslims had been victorious in Khaybar. When the Prophet met his dear cousin Jafar after so many years, the Prophet said, "By Allah, I do not know which occasion pleases me more, the victory at Khaybar or the arrival of Jafar."

Once settled in Medina, Asma visited Hafsa bint Umar. Her father, Umar, asked, "Who is this?" She said, "Asma bint Umays." Umar replied, "The woman who emigrated to Abyssinia by sea." Asma said, "Yes". Then Umar said, "We emigrated before you [to Medina]. Therefore, we are closer to him [the Prophet] than you." Asma was deeply hurt and angry, telling Umar, "No, by Allah. While you lived beside the Messenger, eating and listening to his sermons, we lived far away in a foreign land in Abyssinia. This was for the sake of Allah and His Messenger." She added, "We suffered, and we were scared. By Allah, I will never eat or drink until I mention this to the Messenger of Allah."

Asma told the Prophet what Umar had said. The Prophet asked, "What was your reply?" Asma told him what she had said, and the Messenger of Allah said, "He is not closer to me than you and the emigrants to Abyssinia. He migrated only once, but you and the people of the ship emigrated twice" (Bukhari). Asma was delighted with the Prophet's response. The Muslims who had emigrated to Abyssina and again to Medina, came to Asma asking her what the Prophet said. Asma reported, "I saw Abu Musa and the people of the ship coming one after the other to ask about this hadith. They were very happy to hear the compliment from the Prophet."

Asma, having faced the challenges of two emigrations, was about to stand a greater test – the devastating loss of her husband. It was during the battle of Mutah in 629, between the Muslims and the Byzantine forces. This war was launched to avenge the murder of the Muslim emissary, Harith ibn 'Umayr al-Azdi, who had taken a letter to the king of Basra inviting him to Islam. Al-Harith was attacked and killed by an ally of the Romans. The Muslim army consisted of just 3,000 soldiers while the Romans and their allies far outnumbered them, boasting an army of more than 100,000 men.

The Prophet appointed Jafar as one of the three leaders of the battle, who fell one after the other. Jafar had both his arms brutally cut off while trying to keep the banner of Islam up, and he collapsed in a pool of his own blood, becoming a martyr. For losing his arms in battle, Allah granted him two wings to fly in Paradise. The Messenger henceforth called Jafar, "the owner of two wings".

When she heard the news, Asma was grief-stricken. She lost her friend, her husband and her rock, who had stayed by her side throughout all the difficulties of life. The Prophet ﷺ asked his household to make food for Asma and her children in their affliction (Tirmidhi). Asma's tears did not stop flowing until Allah's Messenger ﷺ visited her on the third day and consoled her.

Asma's son, Abdullah ibn Jafar, relates in the following narration,

> The Messenger of Allah gave Jafar's family some time to mourn him and then visited them and said, "Do not cry over my brother after this day." He then said, "Bring the children of my brother to me." And we were brought to him like young birds. He then said, "Call the barber for me!" And the barber came and shaved our heads. The Messenger of Allah ﷺ held my hand and raised it and said, "O Allah! Be the Supporter of Jafar's family and bless Abdullah [his son] in the transactions of his hands." He said so three times. Then our mother came and mentioned our orphanhood and started crying. The Messenger of Allah then told her, "Asma, are you afraid of poverty for them while I am their guardian in this world and in the Hereafter?"

Asma held fast to her faith and remained patient, devoting her life to her children. The Messenger of Allah ﷺ never forgot Asma or her sons. He would visit them whenever he could, asking after them and showing them kindness. Asma's situation was about to change. The Prophet's closest friend, Abu Bakr was a widower, having just lost his wife, Umm Romaan. The Prophet ﷺ married Asma to Abu Bakr, and they lived together in contentment. When they were blessed with a son, they named him Muhammad. Abu Bakr had great love and esteem for his wife, which was clearly demonstrated when he became ill towards the end of his life, as he requested that Asma wash him when he died.

After a bereavement period, Asma married another caliph of Islam, Ali ibn Abu Talib ﷺ. Ali married Asma after the death of Fatima ﷺ, and they had two sons together, Yahya and Awn.

There was once a quarrel between two sons of Asma. One was Jafar's son and the other was Abu Bakr's son, and each one boasted their father was the better man. Ali called Asma to judge between them, and with great wisdom and diplomacy she said, "I have never seen among the Arabs a young man better than Jafar nor an older man better than

Abu Bakr." The boys stopped their arguing, embraced each other and went on playing again. But Ali jokingly said, "What about me, Asma?" She intelligently replied, "If someone like you is the least of three good people, they will all be elite."

Years later, when Asma heard the news of the death of her son, Muhammad ibn Abu Bakr, the grief adversely affected her body, which was already weak and aging. She was said to have bled from her breasts before passing away to join her son.

Asma bint Umays had survived two migrations, married two caliphs and lived a long life of patience and devotion, may Allah be pleased with her.

AL-SHIFA BINT ABDULLAH

Al-Shifa bint Abdullah al-Qurashiyah al-'Adawiyah was a learned and intelligent woman from the tribe of Quraysh. At a time when the Arabs of Mecca could barely read and write, she excelled in literacy. She is said to be the first female teacher in Islam and the first Muslim woman to hold public office. She embraced Islam before the Hijra and was among the early Muslim women who emigrated from Mecca to Medina to give the pledge of faith to the Prophet ﷺ. She gained her name al-Shifa, meaning "the healer", because she had knowledge in healing and folk medicine.

Once she entered Islam, she ﷺ shouldered the task of educating Muslim women, among her students was Hafsa bint Umar ibn al-Khattab, the Prophet's ﷺ wife.

The Messenger of Allah ﷺ asked al-Shifa to teach Hafsa ﷺ how to write and to train her in healing. Al-Shifa was also famous for knowing words of protection in the pre-Islamic period. After she had embraced Islam and migrated to Medina, she informed the Prophet ﷺ of the incantations. Al-Shifa said, "Once the Prophet ﷺ entered his home when I was there with Hafsa. He said, 'Teach Hafsa the protective words concerning al-namlah [a type of sore that affect one's forehead] as you taught her how to write.'" (Abu Dawud).

The Prophet ﷺ respected al-Shifa greatly and arranged a house for her when she came to Medina. She, like other Muslim women, loved the Prophet ﷺ and learned many of his sayings. The Prophet's regard for al-Shifa influenced Umar's opinion of her. Impressed by al-Shifa's competence, character and judgement, when Umar became caliph, he appointed al-Shifa bint Abdullah as the public administrator. She was possibly the first Muslim woman to hold office. She oversaw all business practices, ensuring they matched with the rulings, teachings and values of Islam. She is also known to have advised Caliph Umar on many occasions on affairs of state.

After a long life of public service, educating women and training them in medical matters, al-Shifa died twenty years after the Hijra. Her son Masruq became a leader, and her other son Sulayman had two sons named Abu Bakr and Uthman, who, like their grandmother, became narrators of hadiths. May Allah be pleased with al-Shifa bint Abdullah, Islam's first female teacher and first female public administrator.

UMM HAKIM BINT AL-HARITH

Umm Hakim bint al-Harith ibn Hisham ibn al-Mughira was a sharp-witted and wise woman who singlehandedly fought Roman soldiers after her wedding feast. Al-Harith, Umm Hakim's father, gave her to Ikrima ibn Amr ibn Hashim in marriage. Ikrima was the son of the infamous enemy of Islam and was himself one of the leading opponents of the Prophet ﷺ. But it was through Umm Hakim's sagacity, that Ikrima later became an important Muslim leader and companion of the Messenger of Allah ﷺ.

Yet it was not until the victory over Mecca that they embraced Islam. First to become Muslim was Umm Hakim and her father al-Harith, who were so impressed by the graciousness of Prophet Muhammad ﷺ on his peaceful conquest of Mecca that they entered Islam. But Umm Hakim's husband, Ikrima, fled the city and headed towards the sea, thinking he would be killed if he stayed in Mecca after his staunch opposition to the Prophet ﷺ.

Umm Hakim ﷺ desired nothing more than that her husband would also embrace Islam. She went to the Prophet ﷺ asking him to forgive her husband Ikrima, if he entered Islam. The Prophet ﷺ said he would forgive him all his previous enmity. No sooner did she hear the Prophet's decree than she went searching for her husband, hoping to find him before his boat sailed. At long last, she found him and told Ikrima that the Prophet ﷺ had forgiven him.

She then began to tell her husband about the lofty principles of

Islam and how honourable the Prophet ﷺ was when he entered Mecca. Ikrimah listened, speechless, as he heard of the Prophet's mercy.

Umm Hakim's words touched her husband's heart. He returned with her to embrace Islam in the presence of the Prophet ﷺ. He requested the Prophet ﷺ to pray for the forgiveness of his past deeds. Then he said, "O Prophet of Allah, whatever money I have spent in preventing people from coming to the way of Allah, I will spend double the amount in inviting people to the right path. And whatever battles I have fought against Islam I will fight twice that number for the sake of Islam."

Thus, through Umm Hakim's clever actions, Ikrima, a former enemy of Islam, became its champion. He took part in several battles, fighting in Allah's cause until he attained the honour of martyrdom when fighting against the Romans in the battle of Yarmouk. Umm Hakim was deeply afflicted by the death of her beloved husband, but she bore her grief patiently.

In 634, she became engaged to Khalid ibn Said, who had been a great Companion and a prominent leader. Before Khalid was to lead the Muslim troops in the battle, he wanted to consummate his marriage with Umm Hakim. Umm Hakim asked him, "Will you not postpone it until those [the Romans] gathering are defeated?" He said, "I think I will be killed [in battle]." And so Umm Hakim agreed. They consummated their marriage near the bridge that was later known as the Bridge of Umm Hakim. The wedding banquet was held in the morning, yet they barely enjoyed their food when the Romans began their attack in the Battle of Marj al-Saffar. Khalid ibn Said rushed onto the battlefield and fought until he died as a martyr. He died in front of his new bride's eyes.

Umm Hakim spurred into action. She quickly secured her garment and rushed out into battle, avenging the death of her two martyred husbands, Ikrima and Khalid. She fought like a lioness and single handedly killed seven Roman soldiers with the pole of her wedding tent.

The Muslims were victorious, and Umm Hakim emerged as a heroine. She later married the caliph of Islam, Umar ibn al-Khattab and they had a daughter named Fatima. Umm Hakim ؓ, the wife of the two martyrs, was a woman respected for her intelligence and her fierce loyalty to all the men she loved.

HIND BINT UTBAH

The story of Hind bint Utbah ibn Rabia ﷺ is one of extraordinary transformation. It is best put in the words of her son, Muawiya ibn Abu Sufyan, who said of his mother, "She was dangerous in the pre-Islamic period but was of good character under Islam". Hind was a bold and confident woman of eloquence, zeal and determination. She was one of the earliest enemies of the Prophet ﷺ and dedicated herself to defeating Islam.

Hind ﷺ was married to al-Fakiha ibn al-Mughira and they had a child named Abban. After separating from al-Fakiha, she married Sakhr ibn Harb, more commonly known as Abu Sufyan – the leader of the Quraysh who shared her passionate enmity against the Prophet ﷺ.

She and Abu Sufyan had three children including a son, Muawiya, who was destined to be the caliph of the Umayyad dynasty. In the battle of Badr, she was afflicted with a triple loss – the deaths of her father Utbah, her brother al-Walid and her uncle Shayba. She bitterly lamented their fall in battle and she hungered for vengeance. When the battle of Uhud arrived, she, along with many other women, accompanied the army of the Quraysh and beat drums and recited poems to encourage the warriors.

It was during this battle that Hind committed a grotesque crime against the lion of Islam, Hamza. She encouraged the slave Wahshi ibn Harb to kill Hamza in revenge for killing her family members in the Battle of Badr. Wahshi sought out Hamza in the clamour of fighting and struck him with his spear. Hamza fell to the ground and died. After the battle, Hind and the other women went to mutilate the corpses of the dead Muslims, cutting off their noses and ears to make them into necklaces and anklets. Hind gave hers to Wahshi. She came to Hamza's corpse and cut out his liver and sunk her teeth into the bloodied organ. She was unable to swallow the bite and spat it out. From that moment, she was called "the liver eater". Then she climbed a rock and shrieked at the top of her voice,

> We have paid you back for Badr
> And a war that follows a war is always violent.
> I could not bear the loss of Utbah
> Nor my brother and his uncle and my first-born.

I have slaked my vengeance and fulfilled my vow.
You, O Wahshi, have assuaged the burning in my breast.
I shall thank Wahshi as long as I live
Until my bones rot in the grave. (Ibn Ishaq)

When the Prophet ﷺ heard what had happened to his uncle Hamza, his grief was so severe that he could not stop weeping. Abdullah ibn Mas'ud narrated that, "We have never seen the Messenger of Allah weeping so much as he was for Hamza bin Abdul Muttalib. He directed him towards the qibla, then he stood at his funeral and sobbed his heart out."

Yet even the strong hatred and vengeance of Hind was cooled by Allah's will. The Prophet's peaceful conquest of Mecca astonished Hind and her husband, Abu Sufyan. They were overpowered not by his revenge, but by his ﷺ mercy. Abu Sufyan embraced Islam before his wife, and he cried to his tribe, "O people of Quraysh, Muhammad sent troops that you could not oppose. Whoever enters Abu Sufyan's house is safe, and whoever stays home or enters the Sacred Mosque is safe."

Hind was still not completely convinced and mocked her husband for embracing Islam. But on the second day of the conquest, she had a turn of heart and asked him to take her to the Prophet ﷺ. "You did not wish to do that yesterday." She replied, "I have never seen such worship of Allah as I did the worship of the Muslims last night. They spent the entire night praying, kneeling and prostrating."

Abu Sufyan worried that her vengeful act against the Prophet's uncle Hamza would upset the Prophet ﷺ, so he suggested that she take some of her relatives with her. Therefore, she gathered some women and requested that one of the Prophet's closest companions, Uthman ibn Affan, accompany her.

Fearing the Prophet's retribution and also feeling shame over her past action, Hind veiled herself so that she would not be recognised. She stood before the Prophet ﷺ and declared, "O Messenger of Allah, praise be to Allah who made the belief He chose manifest. I declare that I believe in Allah and His Messenger." Then she uncovered her face and said, "I am Hind bint Utbah." The Prophet ﷺ, full of grace and mercy, did not utter a word about the treatment of his relative. Instead, he simply said "welcome" to Hind bint Utbah and treated his former enemy with respect and dignity. Hind ؓ said, "By Allah, there was no house on earth that I wanted to destroy more than your house. Now, there is no house on earth that I so dearly wish to honour and raise in glory than yours."

Hind then said, "May we shake hands?" The Prophet ﷺ said, "I do not shake women's hands. What I say to a woman is valid to a hundred" (Muwatta). When Hind returned home, the first thing she did was to break the idol into pieces. With every blow she struck upon it, she exclaimed, "I was deceived by you."

Hind now redirected her fervour and loyalty in the way of Islam. This staunch woman who used to recite poetry to encourage soldiers fighting against the Prophet ﷺ, now sang verses that raised the morale of the Muslim soldiers. Hind, together with Asma bint Abi Bakr, were instrumental in the battle of Yarmouk that saw the Muslim troops outnumbered but with the help of the women, they defeated the Byzantine army.

At one point in the battle, Abu Sufyan, who was being attacked with a shower of arrows, tried to turn his horse away from the enemy. Hind, with the strongest mettle of faith, struck her husband's horse with a tent pole and said, "Where do you think you're going, O Sakhr? Go back into battle and do your best until you compensate for having incited people against Muhammad in the past." An arrow later hit Abu Sufyan in the eye and he became blind.

Hind ؓ had transformed from being a bitter enemy of the Prophet ﷺ into a devoted champion of Islam. Having embraced the pure light of faith, whenever her name is mentioned, we invoke Allah's pleasure on her. Hind ؓ died soon after the battle of Yarmouk in 636, fourteen years after the Hijra.

UMM SHAREEK

Umm Shareek, formerly known as Ghaziyya bint Jabir ibn Hakim, was a Qurayshi woman of nobility and a devoted caller to Islam. After she became a Muslim, she secretly worked non-stop to spread the faith among the women of Quraysh without any concern of the consequences she might face if she was discovered. When she was finally found out by the Meccan pagans, they said, "We will not torture you, for the sake of your kin. All we can do is to return you to them." But her own kin swore that they would torture her.

Umm Shareek related what happened in her own words,

> They carried me on the worst of their camels and left me without water in the middle of the day when the sun was very hot, and they left me alone without shelter. I was about to lose my senses. They kept this up for three days. On the third day, they offered to release me on the condition that I repudiate Islam. But I would not. I merely pointed with my finger skyward. All of sudden, I found a goblet of water near my lips. After I drank from it, the goblet flew back and was suspended in the sky. This happened to me three times. When they noticed my wet face, they were astonished and asked me, "O opponent of Allah, how did you get water?" "It is Allah's sustenance," I replied. They checked their water carrier but found it as it was. Upon seeing this [miracle] they said, "We testify that your Lord and ours is one." They all embraced Islam and migrated to Medina.

Umm Shareek continued to live a life of steadfast piety and guided many women and men to the path of Islam.

UMM AL-FADL

Lubaba bint al-Harith ibn Hazan ibn Bujayr, also known by her nickname Umm al-Fadl, was the second woman after the noble Khadija to embrace Islam. Umm al-Fadl was connected to the Prophet in several ways. She was married to the Prophet's uncle, al-Abbas ibn Abdul-Muttalib, she was sister to Maymuna, the mother of the believers, and she nursed the Prophet's granddaughter.

She and Maymuna also had two half-sisters, Asma and Salama, daughters of 'Umays. The Messenger of Allah described these four sisters as, "The believing sisters". Umm al-Fadl visited Khadija and the Prophet regularly to learn about Islam. Although her husband was not yet Muslim, al-Abbas defended his nephew and honoured their blood ties.

Umm al-Fadl fervently wished that her husband would embrace Islam. She knew that he cherished his status among the Quraysh and that he dealt in usury, but she longed for the day he would turn to the true faith. She was moritifed when, at the Battle of Badr, she saw her husband, the Prophet's own uncle, fight with the Quraysh against the Muslims. Al-Abbas was taken captive, but through the Prophet's mercy he was released. Al-Abbas was moved by his nephew's graciousness, and the light of faith began to enter his heart.

The day Umm al-Fadl dreamed of finally arrived when al-Abbas pronounced his belief in the One God and in the Prophet ﷺ as His Messenger. Umm al-Fadl's home was now a place of harmony and served as refuge for the weak and the poor who could not afford to migrate to escape the persecution of the Quraysh.

Umm al-Fadl was also a very brave woman who fought injustice with her own hands. Her husband's servant, Abu Rafi, narrates that when he heard news of the Muslims' victory at the Battle of Badr, he could not contain his joy. Abu Lahab, a ferocious enemy of Islam, was enraged at the defeat and assaulted him, but Umm al-Fadl came to his rescue. Abu Rafi narrates the story,

> I was a weak man carving cups near the well of Zamzam. While I was sitting there with Umm al-Fadl, we heard of the victory and were very pleased. Abu Lahab was enraged. Later on, Abu Sufyan came, and Abu Lahab said to him, "Will you tell us what happened in Badr?" Abu Sufyan said, "We did nothing but give the Muslims our backs to kill us or to capture us as they liked. By God, I did not blame our troops because the people we met were different. They were white and riding on white horses. By God, they could not be opposed." Thereupon, Abu Rafi raised the curtain of the room where he was working and said, "Those must have been angels."

Abu Lahab knocked Abu Rafi to the ground and pinned him down, continuing to violently beat him. Umm al-Fadl grabbed a tent pole and struck Abu Lahab fiercely on the head and said angrily, "You consider him weak in the absence of his master?" Abu Lahab then turned away humiliated. Abu Lahab's wound became infected and he died a week later.

Umm al-Fadl remained in Mecca until after the treaty of Hudaybiya, when she and her family migrated to Medina. When in Medina, as was her habit in Mecca, Umm al-Fadl maintained her frequent visits to the Prophet's house. She not only visited her sister Maymuna's house but also the homes of all the Prophet's wives. They honoured and respected her, regarding her as a woman of excellence.

One night, Umm al-Fadl had a dream and came to the Messenger of Allah seeking his interpretation. She said, "Messenger of Allah, I saw in my dream that a part of your body was in my house." The Prophet ﷺ then answered her, "Fatima [my daughter] will give birth to a boy whom you will nurse with the milk of Quthm [meaning her son]." When Fatima gave birth to al-Husayn, Umm al-Fadl nursed him along with her own son Quthm.

Once, Umm al-Fadl carried al-Husayn to his grandfather ﷺ, and he cuddled and kissed him until the boy urinated on him. Umm al-Fadl smacked him between his shoulders, but the Prophet ﷺ rebuked her, "You have hurt my son. May Allah have mercy on you." Then he sprayed water over the wet area and said to Umm al-Fadl, "Wash the affected place if it is urination of a female baby and spray it with water if it is from a male baby."

Umm al-Fadl had the great honour of performing the farewell pilgrimage with the Prophet ﷺ along with her husband al-Abbas and her children. On the day of Arafat, the Companions were debating whether the Prophet ﷺ was fasting or not, and many refused to break their own fasts out of uncertainty. Umm al-Fadl decided to take a vessel of milk to the Messenger of Allah ﷺ who drank from it. Through this simple, wise act of Umm al-Fadl, the Companions were now enlightened and those who were fasting broke their fasts. Umm al-Fadl had no doubt heard from the Messenger of Allah ﷺ that it is not permissible for a pilgrim to fast on the day of Arafat and she has given generations of Muslims the evidence by her deed.

Umm al-Fadl ﷺ reported thirty hadiths of the Prophet ﷺ. During her lifetime, she showed independent leadership, compassion and bravery. She died during the caliphate of Uthman ibn Affan ﷺ, may Allah be pleased with the courageous and pious Umm al-Fadl.

AL-RUBAI BINT MUAWIDH

Al-Rubai bint Muawidh ibn al-Harith ﷺ was an honourable and knowledgeable woman whom the Companions would seek out to ask questions on matters of belief. She was from among the Ansar who gave their pledge of faith to the Prophet ﷺ beneath the tree, a pledge mentioned in the glorious Quran,

> Prophet, when believing women come and pledge to you that they will not ascribe any partner to God, nor steal, nor commit adultery, nor kill their children, nor lie about who has fathered their children, nor disobey you in any righteous thing, then you should accept their pledge of allegiance and pray to God to forgive them. God is most forgiving and merciful." (Quran 60:12)

It is to Al-Rubai that we owe our understanding of ablution, for she reported the hadith concerning the manner of the Prophet's wudu. Abu Dawud reported on the authority of al-Rubai that she said, "The Prophet used to visit us. Once he asked for some water to do ablution." She then described the Prophet's way of doing ablution saying, "He started by washing his hands three times." Al-Rubai also gave us a window into a beautiful scene at her wedding feast. She narrated,

At my wedding banquet, the Prophet ﷺ came and sat on my bed. The girls began to sing and lament their fathers who died in the Battle of Badr. One of the girls sang, "And we have a Prophet who knows what will happen tomorrow." The Prophet ﷺ said, "Do not say that. It would be better to sing what you said before that." (Bukhari).

Al-Rubai was herself no stranger to the battlefield. She was among the Muslim women who carried water to the soldiers and treated the wounded. She also courageously fought against the enemy when times were critical.

Al-Rubai ﷺ died during the era of Muawiya, forty-five years after the Hijra. May Allah have mercy on her soul.

AL-KHANSA

Al Khansa, known also as Tamadur bint Amr ibn al-Harith ibn al-Sharid, was a very famous and highly eloquent poet. She belonged to the tribe of Banu Sulaym, a tribe that dominated part of the Hejaz in the pre-Islamic era. Al-Khansa was very beautiful, well-mannered and wonderfully articulate. She started reciting poems very early in her life but did not go beyond two or three lines of poetry when tragedy hit her family.

It was her sorrow over the death of her brother Sakhr that surfaced her innate talent, and she began to recite long, emotional and poignant poems to eulogize him. One of her surviving poems reads, "O my eyes, shed tears generously! Will you not weep for Sakhr, the generous?" Her brother's death led to her composing masterpieces that turned her into the greatest poet in the genre of lamentations. It is a consensus of the scholars of poetry that no woman ever attained the status of al-Khansa in poetry, neither before her nor after her.

Al-Khansa ﷺ went to Medina along with a delegation from Banu Sulaym, where she embraced Islam and pledged allegiance to the Messenger of Allah ﷺ. The Prophet ﷺ admired her poetry greatly and used to appeal to her to recite more by calling her "O Khanas!" a way of shortening her name to show his fondness for her talent.

In addition to being a great poet, al-Khansa was also a brave warrior. She accompanied the Muslim soldiers with her four children in the battle of al-Qadisiyya against the army of the Sasanian Empire in 636. Before entering the battle, she inspired valour in her sons' hearts, saying,

> My sons! You embraced Islam and migrated willingly. By Allah besides Whom there is no other deity worthy of being worshipped, you are all sons of one man as you are sons of one woman. I have never cheated on your father. Never have I brought disgrace upon your uncle, disparaged your esteem or altered your lineage. You know the great and abundant reward that Allah has set aside for the Muslims who fight against the disbelievers. Know that the everlasting abode is better than this transient one. Allah says, "You who believe, be steadfast, more steadfast than others, be ready, always be mindful of God, so that you may prosper." [Quran 3:200] When you wake up tomorrow morning sound and healthy by Allah's leave, go and fight against your enemy with sure understanding and seek Allah's help over His enemies. When you see that the war has become tense, engage yourselves in the fight gallantly and resiliently that you may attain treasures and honour in the Abode of Eternity.

Filled with courage and enthusiasm, al-Khansa's sons threw themselves into battle, until they attained martyrdom, one by one, on the battlefield. When informed of their deaths, al-Khansa said, "Praise be to Allah who honoured me with their martyrdom. I pray to Allah to let me accompany them on the Last Day." She ﷺ did not lament them as she did before when her brother, Sakhr, died. She was patient and sought Allah's reward.

Al-Khansa died in the era of Uthman ibn Affan, twenty-four years after the Hijra. May Allah have mercy on the great poet and warrior.

KHAWLA BINT THALABA

Khawla bint Thalaba ibn Asram ibn Auf, was an Ansari woman from the Medinan tribe of Khazraj. She was strong minded, stood up for her rights and even had the title of a Quranic *surah* referenced to her. Khawla ﷺ was the wife of Anas ibn al-Samit, who had fought alongside the Prophet ﷺ in Badr, Uhud, and many other battles.

Once Khawla ﷺ argued with her husband and he retorted with the pagan expression known as *zihar*, "You are to me as the back of my mother." In pagan customs, this statement implied a divorce and freed the husband from any conjugal duties. The custom was degrading to women, and it was particularly hard on Khawla, for she loved her husband and they had young children. Without Anas, she had no resources to support them.

Khawla took her plea to the Prophet ﷺ, but he could not rule on the case as he was not directed by Allah about this custom. The Prophet said, "I have no ruling concerning that. I think you are divorced." Khawla had only one way to turn – towards Allah. She begged her Creator for help, and Allah responded to her supplication.

No sooner did she finish her prayer than Jibril ﷺ come to the Prophet ﷺ. After he had recovered from the visitation, he said, "O Khawla, Allah has revealed some verses of the Quran concerning you and your husband." Then he started to recite,

> God has heard the words of the woman who disputed with you [Prophet] about her husband and complained to God, God has heard what you both had to say. He is all hearing, all seeing. He is all hearing, all seeing. Even if any of you say to their wives, "You are to me like my mother's back," they are not their mothers, their only mothers are those who gave birth to them. What they say is certainly blameworthy and false, but God is pardoning and forgiving. Those of you who say

such a thing to their wives, then go back on what they have said, must free a slave before the couple may touch one another again – this is what you are commanded to do, and God is fully aware of what you do. Anyone who does not have the means should fast continuously for two months before they touch each other, and anyone unable to do this should feed sixty needy people. This is so that you may [truly] have faith in God and His Messenger ﷺ. These are the bounds set by God. Grievous torment awaits those who ignore them. (Quran 58:1–5)

These verses appear in the chapter known as al-Mujadila, 'The Dispute' or 'The Pleading Woman'. Khawla's plea was accepted and henceforth, this derogatory custom was abolished. Aisha said, "Praise be to Allah Who hears all sounds. The woman who pleaded with the Prophet ﷺ came and spoke with him in one corner of my house. I did not hear her but Allah did and revealed [the ayah]."

Even upon the revelation, Khawla's love and loyalty for her husband did not falter, and this only raised her in dignity. According to Ibn Kathir's *tafsir* (exegesis), when the Prophet ﷺ said to Khawla, "Command him (her husband) to free a slave." Khawla replied, "O Allah's Messenger! He does not have any to free." Then the Prophet ﷺ said, "Let him fast for two consecutive months." Khawla replied, "By Allah! He is an old man and cannot fast." Then he said, "Let him feed sixty poor people with dates." Khawla said, "Oh Allah's Messenger! By Allah, he does not have any of that." The Prophet said, "We will help him with a basket of dates." Khawla replied, "And I, O Allah's Messenger! I will help him with another."

The Prophet ﷺ said, "You have done a righteously good thing, so go and give away the dates on his behalf and take care of your cousin." And she did just that.

Khawla did not even shy away from admonishing the imposing and mighty Umar. Once, under his caliphate, she blocked Umar's way in order to advise him. She said, "O Umar, fear Allah in your people. You have to know that whoever fears the warning will find the remotest thing close. Whoever fears death would not like to miss anything. Whoever believes in the Judgement will fear torture." One of Umar's companions told her to stop speaking this way to the caliph, and said, "It is too much, and this is the leader of the believers," Umar said, "Let her be. Do you not know her? This is Khawla to whom Allah listened from above the seven heavens. Surely, Umar should listen too."

Khawla's story demonstrated that women were to be treated with respect and justice by their husbands, and it shows that Khawla had the presence of mind and the conviction to address the caliph. May Allah have mercy on Khawla bint Thalaba.

UMM ROMAAN

Umm Romaan, the mother of Aisha bint Abi Bakr ☙, was a courteous, sincere, generous and beautiful woman. She was the daughter of Amir ibn Uwaymir and the honoured mother-in-law to the Prophet ☙. Umm Romaan was born in a region called al-Sara in the Arabian Peninsula. She first married al-Harith ibn Sakhira and they had a child named al-Tufayl.

She ☙ migrated with her husband to Mecca before the advent of Islam where they allied with Abu Bakr al-Siddiq, one of the eminent figures in Quraysh. Shortly afterward, al-Harith died. As was the custom, Abu Bakr offered protection to the widow and proposed to Umm Romaan in honour of his friend al-Harith. Umm Romaan married Abu Bakr and they had two children, Abdul-Rahman and Aisha ☙.

No sooner was Muhammad sent as a messenger than Abu Bakr followed him. He was the first man to enter Islam. Umm Romaan, like her husband, readily embraced Islam and she stood by her husband in times of adversity, when the Muslims suffered torture and persecution.

The Prophet ☙ visited the house of his greatest friend every day, and Umm Romaan always received the Prophet with the utmost care and hospitality. When Khawla bint Hakim brought news to Umm Romaan of the Prophet's proposal to Aisha, she was overjoyed, knowing that their union would bring great blessings.

Before the marriage was consummated in Medina, Aisha had been adversely affected by the weather and became weak, thin and pale. Umm Rooman lavished care on her daughter until she regained her health, feeding her cucumber with fresh dates so that she would enter the Prophet's household a healthy, glowing bride.

Years later, when Aisha was accused falsely of adultery, Umm Romaan's motherly love shone through again. She was pained by the slander of her daughter and sought to protect Aisha by not telling her of the awful gossip. Umm Romaan held on to her deep faith and begged Allah to disclose the innocence of her daughter. When Aisha discovered the rumour herself, she went home and blamed her mother for not telling her. Umm Romaan only said, "O daughter, do not worry. By Allah, the more beloved and beautiful a wife is to her husband, the more rumours the people will circulate."

Eventually after a month had passed, Allah revealed the innocence of Aisha in the glorious Quran. But the anxiety for her innocent child took its toll on Umm Romaan and she fell very ill. Now it was Aisha's turn to look after her mother, nursing her until she died. The Prophet ﷺ entered her grave and asked Allah to forgive her by saying, "O Allah, You know well what Umm Romaan suffered for Your sake and the sake of Your Messenger."

He also paid honour to her purity, modesty and heavenly beauty that qualified her to be among the wide-eyed women of Paradise. While she was being lowered into her grave, the Prophet ﷺ said, "Let him who wants to see a woman among the beautiful women of Paradise who have wide and lovely eyes, look at Umm Romaan."

May Allah have mercy on Umm Romaan, the mother of the mother of the believers.

NUSSAIBAH BINT KA'AB (UMM AMARA)

Nusayba bint Kaab ibn Amr ibn Auf al-Ansariyya, also known as Umm Amara, was a courageous warrior who gained the honorary title "the Prophet's shield" for defending the Messenger ﷺ on the battlefield.

Umm Amara was among the first women of Medina to enter Islam. She accompanied the delegation that set out from Medina for Mecca to give the pledge of faith to the Prophet ﷺ. The delegation consisted of seventy-two people, of whom two were women. Umm Amara was a young newlywed when she had the honour of meeting the Prophet ﷺ in the middle of the night at Aqaba.

Umm Amara fought in all the greatest battles in early Islam. She had not intended to fight but initially accompanied the Muslim army, along with her husband and her two sons Abdullah and Habib, to carry water to the soldiers and tend to the wounded. But during the battle of Uhud, when she witnessed how the Muslims were being trapped and the Prophet ﷺ was in danger, she took up a discarded sword and rushed to the Prophet's ﷺ side to defend him alongside her husband and two sons. Together, the family guarded the Prophet ﷺ from danger.

Umm Amara fought valiantly and recounts the tale of the battle in her own words,

> In the battle of Uhud, I saw the people leaving the Prophet ﷺ alone. There were only ten people around him. Subsequently, I stood by him beside my two sons and my husband. Many people passed by the Prophet ﷺ defeated. Meanwhile, the Prophet ﷺ noticed me unarmed. When he noticed a man fleeing from the battlefield with his weapon, he ordered him, "Throw your weapon to someone who can fight instead." After he threw it, I picked it up and started to defend the Prophet ﷺ. But the horsemen trapped us and put us into difficulty. Were they infantry like us, we would have defeated them if Allah willed it. Thereupon, a horseman attacked me. But I received his sword on my shield, and when he turned back, I hit the rear of his horse with my sword. The man fell down on his back. Then the Prophet ﷺ shouted, "O son of Umm Amara, your mother, your mother!" Then came my son to help me and I killed the man. I engaged in fighting and protected the Messenger of Allah with the sword while at the same time shooting arrows until I was wounded.

Abdullah ibn Zayed, her son, was wounded during the battle and he bled profusely. His mother ran to him and bandaged his wounds, and then commanded him, "Go and fight the people, my son!" The Prophet ﷺ looked at Umm Amara in admiration of her bravery and sacrifice and said, "From where can anyone get courage like you, O Umm Amara?"

At one time, the enemy closed in on the Prophet ﷺ and struck Umm Amara with a blow to her neck, leaving a serious wound. The Prophet ﷺ quickly called on her son, "Your mother! Your mother! Bind her wound! May Allah bless you, the people of a house! The stand of your mother is better than the stand of so-and-so. May Allah have mercy on you, people of a house!"

Umm Amara, seeing the Prophet's concern for her wound and admiration for her valour, earnestly requested him, "Ask Allah to make us your companions in the Garden!" So he said, "O Allah, make them my companions in Paradise." This is all Umm Amara desired, and she replied, "I do not care what afflicts me in this world!"

Umar ibn al-Khattab ؓ narrates that the Messenger of Allah said, "Whenever I turned left or right on the day of the battle of Uhud, I always saw her [Umm Amara] fighting to defend me." Umm Amara, the Prophet's shield, received about thirteen wounds in the battle.

As the years passed, this fearless woman kept on serving the call of Islam in times of war and peace. Umm Amara, aside from being an exceptional warrior, also had an excellent memory and was a narrator of hadiths. Some of her narrations contain *fiqh* and Islamic legal rulings.

For example, at-Tirmidhi, an-Nasa'i and Ibn Majah reported in their Sunan on the authority of Umm Amara that the Messenger of Allah ﷺ visited her and presented her with food. The Prophet ﷺ told her, "Eat." She said, "I am fasting." The Prophet ﷺ then said, "If food is eaten in the house of a fasting person, the angels will invoke blessing on them."

The Prophet ﷺ sent Umm Amara's son, Habib, as an envoy to Musaylama the Liar of the Banu Hanifa clan. Musaylama was called "the liar" because he falsely claimed prophethood. Habib was the younger of Umm Amara's two sons from her first husband, Zayd ibn Asim. Habib was gentle hearted but firm in his faith. When Habib delivered the message and fulfilled the trust assigned to him, Musaylama asked him, "Do you believe that Muhammad is the Messenger of Allah?" He answered in the affirmative. Musaylama then said, "Do you believe that I am a Messenger of Allah?" Habib's denial enraged Musaylama. He tried to force Habib to turn his back on the Prophet ﷺ and Allah, but all his attempts were in vain. He tied Habib up and had him tortured, cutting off his limbs piece by piece. But Habib held fast to his faith and the pleasure of Allah until he died from the mutilation to his body.

When Umm Amara heard of the terrible manner of her son's death, she vowed that she would take her revenge and that she would witness and take part in the killing of Musaylama the Liar. After the Prophet's death, Abu Bakr and Umar ؓ often visited Umm Amara to assure, console and honour her. The opportunity for justice finally came at the battle of Yamama. Umm Amara asked Abu Bakr's permission to fight. Abu Bakr ؓ said to her, "We know that you fight well. You can go (may Allah bless you)." Umm Amara was now ageing and becoming weak, but she held the fire of faith in her heart and sought the honour of martyrdom.

She set out to fight, accompanied by her other son, Abdullah. Side by side, they pushed their way through the rows of soldiers, looking for Habib's murderer. Umm Amara sustained multiple wounds, including her hand being cut off, but still she persisted in the battle.

Abdullah managed to take Musaylama down aided by Wahshi ibn Harb, the man who had killed Hamza, the Prophet's uncle. Umm Amara came to Musaylama who was lying in the ground wounded with Wahshi's javelin. Umm Amara started striking him with a spear until he died. Then she prostrated to Allah. She ﷺ survived the battle but her son Abdullah had fallen as a martyr.

Umm Amara ﷺ stands as a beacon of courage and sacrifice to women and men throughout the centuries. May Allah have mercy on this lionhearted warrior woman.

UMM MIHJAN

Very little is known about Umm Mihjan ﷺ, but whatever little we have is a beautiful testament to a good-hearted, simple woman whose greatness lay in her humility. Umm Mihjan was a poor woman who lived in Medina and regularly swept the mosque. Although she was old and weak, she took the greatest effort in cleaning the mosque, which was the hub of the Muslim community. She volunteered to undertake this task on a daily basis without expecting anything, she only sought the pleasure of her Sustainer.

The Prophet ﷺ was always very kind to her. One morning, the Prophet ﷺ did not see her and he asked his Companions about her. They said, "She died and was buried." The Prophet ﷺ asked why he was not informed of her death. Abu Huraira said that they may have thought she was not important enough. The Prophet ﷺ said, "Will you lead me to her grave?" There, he performed the funeral prayer and said, "These graves are full of a darkness that engulfs their dwellers, but Allah enlightens them by the virtue of my prayers" (Bukhari and Muslim)

He then continued to say that he had seen this woman and she had dust of the mosque in her hands and was standing in Paradise. Seeing how the Prophet ﷺ reacted to her death and hearing her words, the Companions realised how great Umm Mihjan truly was.

May Allah bless Umm Mihjan, who cleaned the mosque and was given Paradise.

UMM HANI AND NAB'A

Umm Hani, also known as Fakhita bint Abi Talib, was Ali ibn Abu Talib's sister. While Umm Hani had embraced Islam, her husband held on to the old religion, but she remained with him and their children in Mecca, instead of migrating with the Muslims.

Umm Hani is mentioned along with Nab'a, her Abyssinian maid, since the hadith about a key episode in the Prophet's life – the Night Journey – revolved around them both. While there are many narrations about the Night Journey from other Companions, Umm Hani's narration has many chains. As for Nab'a, she was the link and a trusted source of the narration. Ibn Hajar said that after the Prophet's Night Journey, he was about to go and inform the people of his experience when Umm Hani took the edge of his garment, revealing his stomach that was as white as folded Egyptian fabric, and told him, "O Prophet of Allah, do not tell the people this, in case they disbelieve you and harm you." But he said, "By Allah, I will tell them."

Umm Hani then instructed Nab'a to follow him and report back on what he told people and how they responded. Nab'a was an astute woman, with an excellent memory and an open heart. With sincerity and honesty, she narrated the conversation that took place between the Messenger of Allah and a group from the Quraysh.

There is an account in Umm Hani's life that demonstrates her sense of honour and compassion. On the day of the conquest of Mecca, one of the polytheists escaped to Umm Hani's house seeking her protection. Her brother, Ali ibn Abi Talib followed the man to her house, but Umm Hani stood between them, preventing Ali from hurting the man. An argument broke between brother and sister, and at that moment, the Messenger of Allah arrived. When he heard what Umm Hani had to say, he honoured her right of giving protection and said, "We have given protection to those you have given protection to, Umm Hani."

May Allah have mercy on Umm Hani for her mercy and on her Abyssian maid, Nab'a.

UMM MA'BAD

Umm Ma'bad was an eloquent, generous and strong Bedouin woman, whose real name was Aatika bint Khalid al-Khuza'iyyah. Umm Ma'bad is connected to one of the most extraordinary events in the Prophet's life - the Hijrah from Mecca to Medina.

Umm Ma'bad had a camp in an area called Qudayd. She would sit wrapped up in her cloak in the courtyard of her camp and generously provide food and drink to the travellers passing by.

The Messenger of Allah and his Companions Abu Bakr, Amar ibn Fuhayrah, a freed slave of Abu Bakr and their guide Abdullah ibn Urayqit (who was then a polytheist), stopped to take rest and refreshment in her camp. They asked her for some milk, meat or dates, which they were more than willing to pay for. Umm Ma'bad was saddened that she could not offer them anything, for it was a time of severe drought. She said, "By Allah, if we had anything we would not lack in showing [all of you] hospitality."

The Prophet then saw a frail goat within the shaded side of the camp, which was being kept away from the flock of sheep. The Messenger of Allah asked Umm Ma'bad, "Does this goat have any milk?" Umm Ma'bad answered, "She is too weak to have any." He then said, "Would you allow me to milk her?" She replied, "May my father and mother be ransomed for you, if you see any milk in her you may milk her."

The Prophet then called for the goat and placed her legs between his, gently stroked her udder and mentioned the name of Allah. The udder suddenly swelled with milk. The Prophet asked for a vessel big enough to hold milk for the entire group and began to squeeze milk into it. He then gave Umm Ma'bad and his Companions the goat's milk until everyone was satiated, after which he also drank and said, "The cup-bearer drinks last."

He then milked the goat one more time and once again offered it to all of them. Whereas previously they had gulped down the milk due to their severe thirst, this time they drank slowly. The third time the Prophet milked the goat, he did it exclusively for Umm Ma'bad. Then he and his Companions mounted their camels and moved on.

After they had left, Umm Ma'bad's husband, Aktham ibn Abi al-Jawn al-Khuza'I, returned with his flock of emaciated sheep. He was astonished to see milk in the vessel and asked his wife, "Umm Ma'bad what is this? Where did you get this milk from? There is no goat with milk here!" Umm Ma'bad, who was overwhelmed by the miracle she had just witnessed, replied, "A blessed man passed by us."

Abu Ma'bad asked his wife, "Describe him." What then followed was the most beautiful, elegant and fitting description that we have of the Prophet ﷺ, and it was given by a humble Bedouin woman who had met him ﷺ only briefly. Even Ali ibn Abi Talib, who gave detailed accounts and had spent a long period of time with the Prophet ﷺ, could not match Umm Ma'bad's close observations. She told her husband,

> I saw a man who is distinctly handsome and of a beautiful countenance. He is well-built, neither blemished by a big belly nor disfigured by an unusually small head. The pupils of his eyes are very dark, his eyelashes are very long and the area around the pupils is extremely white. His eyebrows are perfectly close. He has very dark hair, a rather long neck and a thick beard. When he remains silent he is ever contemplative and when he speaks, eminence and splendour exhibit in his words. His words are like sliding stringed pearls. He is a gifted orator whose words are neither too few nor too many. He has the clearest wand and the most audible voice as he speaks. When you look at him from afar, he is the most handsome of all people, and when you move closer to him, he is the most pleasant of them. You will never be tired of looking at him. He is like a branch between two branches.
>
> He is the most handsome of the three [Companions] and the most important of them. He has companions who honour him; when he speaks they listen to his words and when he commands they hasten to carry out his order. They serve and gather around him. He neither frowns nor nags.

Abu Ma'bad exclaimed, "By Allah! This is the man of Quraysh! If I see him, I will follow him." Umm Ma'bad and her husband went to Medina, embraced Islam and swore allegiance to the Prophet ﷺ. Also with them was Umm Ma'bad's brother, known as Khunays (or Hubaysh) ibn Khalid, who reported the account. The Bedouin couple stayed in the Prophet's company as much as they possibly could. Their embrace of Islam and their commitment to the Prophet ﷺ, all resulted from his ﷺ sheer grace and dignity and the miracle of the goat.

According to a report narrated by al-Waqidi and many others, the goat lived for a long time providing abundant milk. Umm Ma'bad's first words about the Prophet ﷺ being a blessed man was nothing but the truth. May Allah be pleased with Umm Mab'ad, the eloquent woman of the desert.

RUFAYDA AL-ASLAMIYA

Rufayda al-Aslamiya ؓ was highly respected for her expertise in medical treatment, particularly on the battlefield. She was born into the Bani Aslam tribe and was among the first people in Medina to embrace Islam and welcome the Prophet ﷺ into the city. Rufayda's father, Saad al-Aslamy, was a physician under whom Rufayda initially obtained clinical experience and trained as an expert healer.

The first mention of Rufayda was during the Battle of the Trench (otherwise known as the Battle of Confederates) when Saad Ibn Muadh ؓ, a prominent Companion, was struck with a spear in the vein in his arm. The Messenger of Allah ﷺ said, "Let him stay in Rufayda's tent in the mosque until I return."

Whenever Rufayda was mentioned, her tent was mentioned too. Rufayda's tent was a kind of 7th century field hospital. There were bandages for dressing wounds, surgical materials and special treatments for pain, and it was all managed by this formidable Ansari woman. Rufayda did not take any wage or seek reward for her work. She used her personal money to care for the soldiers, hoping only for Allah's reward.

Many female Companions who took care of the wounded and gave water to the thirsty soldiers were under her supervision. She had excellent organizational and management skills, and trained other female companions in healthcare. The Prophet ﷺ was so impressed by Rufayda's unit of nurse volunteers that he assigned a share of the bounty to her, which was equivalent to that of the soldiers who had participated in battle.

During times of peace, Rufayda was interested in hygiene and disease prevention, and she tended to orphans, the handicapped and the poor. She developed the first ever documented mobile care units that were able to meet the medical needs of the community.

Allah bless Rufayda al-Aslamiya, Islam's first Muslim nurse and surgeon.

UMM KULTHUM BINT UQBA

Umm Kulthum was among the very first people in Mecca to embrace Islam. Her father, Uqba ibn Abi al-Mu'eet, was a leader of the noble Quraysh. He was also among the cruellest and harshest enemies of the Prophet ﷺ. Umm Kulthum was unmarried when she became Muslim. She was not persecuted and stayed in Mecca until the treaty of Hudaybiya. Yet as soon as the opportunity for migration arose, Umm Kulthum joined the Muslim emigrants setting out for Medina. Ibn Sa'd wrote,

> She was the first person to migrate to Medina after the Prophet's migration. We did not know of any Muslim Qurayshi woman who went out of her parents' house and migrated to Allah and His Messenger, except Umm Kulthum. She went out of Mecca alone and she [later] travelled in the company of a man from Banu Khuza tribe until she arrived at Medina.

But hard at Umm Kulthum's heels were her brothers, Ammara and al-Waleed, who entered Medina only the day after she set foot in the city. They went to the Prophet ﷺ and demanded that their sister be sent back with them. She immediately interjected, "O Messenger of Allah, I am a woman. And women are naturally weak. I fear that [if I am sent back] they might tempt me in my religion, and I might not be able to bear that." So the Messenger of Allah ﷺ rejected her brothers' demand. It was on this occasion that Allah revealed, "You who believe, test the believing women when they come to you as emigrants. God knows best about their faith, and if you are sure of their belief, do not send them back to the disbelievers" (Quran 60:10). These verses appear in the chapter entitled, 'Women Tested', referring to the women who left Mecca to join the Muslims, and Umm Kulthum was among them. Ibn Abbas was asked how the Prophet ﷺ examined the women and he answered, "The Prophet would examine them thus, 'Tell me by Allah, did you migrate because you don't like your husband? Tell me by Allah, did you migrate just because you want to abandon a land for another? Tell me by Allah, did you migrate because of a material of this world that you wish to attain? Tell me by Allah, you did not migrate but for your love for Allah and His Messenger?' " Umm Kulthum passed the test on all levels.

Umm Kulthum's hand was then highly sought in marriage by the Companions. Yet from them all, this lady of the ruling Meccan elite chose to marry a freed slave, Zayd ibn Haritha. After Zayd was martyred in the Battle of Mu'ta, she married Zubayr ibn Awwam, a commander in the army with whom she had a daughter named Zaynab. She was later widowed. After the death of Allah's Messenger ﷺ she married Abdur-Rahman ibn Awf, in accordance with the Prophet's instruction. Abdur-Rahman was one of the ten companions promised Paradise by the Prophet ﷺ.

Umm Kulthum and Abdur-Rahman had two sons, Humayd and Ibrahim. When Abdur-Rahman also died, Amr ibn As, a military commander, married her. But Umm Kulthum died only a month after this marriage.

As well as the Arab custom of protecting widows, Umm Kulthum's repeated marriages indicate how highly she was regarded and sought after because of her piety, morality and status. May Allah be pleased with Umm Kulthum, who migrated to Medina only for Allah and His Messenger ﷺ.

UMM MANI

Umm Mani, or Asma bint Amr, was one of two women in the delegation that came from Medina to Mecca to pledge allegiance to the Messenger of Allah ﷺ. She, along with Umm Amara, witnessed this great pledge which was the turning point in the history of Islam. In '*al-Isaba*', Ibn Hajar writes,

> Umm Mani is the mother of Shubath. Some say her name is Asma bint Amr. Ibn Sa'd reported on the authority of al-Waqidi, who also narrated with his chain of transmission reaching Umm Amara, that she said, "Men were shaking the hand of the Messenger of Allah on the night of al-Aqabah while al-Abbas was holding the Prophet's hand. When it was my turn and that of Umm Mani, my husband, Arabah- ibn Amr said, 'O Messenger of Allah, these are two women who came with us and they also want to pledge their allegiance to you.' The Messenger of Allah responded, 'I have accepted your pledge. I do not shake women's hands.' "

Umm Mani was a patient and courageous woman. During battles, she treated the wounded and gave food and water to thirsty soldiers. The Messenger of Allah ﷺ recognised her efforts and gave her a share of the booty in the campaign of Khaybar.

Umm Mani's greatness was also seen through her son, Muadh, who was renowned for his excellent knowledge of Islam and *fiqh*, highly regarded by everyone around him and, most of all, loved by the Prophet ﷺ who appointed him as governor of Yemen. Umar al-Khattab remarked, "Women were unable to give birth to the like of Muadh!" May Allah be pleased with Umm Mani, a truly, loyal woman and mother of a king among scholars.

SHAYMA BINT HARITH

Shayma was the foster sister of the noble Prophet Muhammad ﷺ. Her mother was Halima bint Abi Dhuhayb, the Prophet's wet nurse. He stayed in their home for the first formative years of his ﷺ life.

Shayma was about five years old when the Prophet ﷺ joined their village household, and she helped her mother with household chores or in the fields. She was old enough to observe that since Muhammad ﷺ was brought into their midst, there was an extraordinary change in the situation of her family, which transformed from hardship to ease. Shayma realized that it was the little Muhammad who was bringing them tremendous blessings.

Shayma adored her little milk-brother. She played with him, looked after him and used to sing to Muhammad while Halima nursed him. Abu 'Urwah al-Azdi reported that she sang the following words of supplication, "Our Lord! Keep Muhammad alive for us so that I can see him become an adolescent then a leader. Suppress his enemies and those who are envious of him and give him an everlasting glory!"

The Prophet ﷺ grew up in an environment of nurture and love for the first five years of his life. He was then taken back to his mother Amina in Mecca and eventually turned into the leader Shayma had mentioned in her song, yet he never forgot the bond he had with his foster family.

Many years later after the conquest of Mecca, the Bedouin tribes of Hawazin, Thaqif, Banu Bakr and others, came together to fight against Muhammad ﷺ in the battle of Hunayn in 630/ 8 AH. They brought together a contingent of more than 30,000 men and went out accompanied by their women and children in response to the demand of their leader Malik ibn Awf.

It was towards the end of this battle that the Prophet ﷺ was unexpectedly reunited with his foster sister. After the Muslims won victory, Shayma was among the captives. She told the Muslims that their master was her brother and asked to be taken to him. They took her to Muhammad ﷺ, and she pleaded, "O Muhammad. I am your sister". The Prophet ﷺ looked at her, a woman of more than seventy years, and asked, "Have you any proof of that?" She replied, "You bit me when I was carrying you in the valley of Sarar. We were there with shepherds. Your father is my father, your mother is my mother."

When the Messenger of Allah ﷺ heard this, he was taken back to his childhood days and fondly remembered his time with his Bedouin family. The Prophet ﷺ spread out his cloak for Shayma and invited her to sit beside him. His eyes filled with tears as Shayma told him that his foster parents, Halima and Harith, had both died in the fullness of their years. He then told her, "If you like, you can stay with me and you will always be loved and honoured, or if you prefer, I can provide for you and send you back to your people." Shayma said she wished to enter Islam but that she would return to her clan. The Prophet ﷺ gave her a rich gift and said he would see her again.

The Prophet's love for his foster sister and the milk they shared from Halima, bound them together through peace and war. May Allah have mercy on Shayma, the Prophet's milk-sister.

KHAWLA BINT AL-AZWAR

Khawla bint al-Azwar was a courageous warrior who fought so valiantly on the battlefield that everyone mistook her for Khalid bin Waleed, who was nicknamed "the sword of Allah".

Khawla was the daughter of one of the chiefs of the Bani Assad tribe, her father's name was either Malik or Tariq bin Aws. Al-Azwar was his nickname. Khawla's family were among the first converts to Islam.

Her brother, Dhirar ibn al-Azwar, who was a Companion of the Prophet ﷺ, was a great commander and an eloquent poet. Khawla and Dhirar had a strong bond, she was her brother's companion wherever he went, and he trained her in swordsmanship and the art of poetry.

During the Battle of Sanita al-Uqab in 634, during the Siege of Damascus, Dhirar was among the commanders of the Muslim forces, but he was wounded and taken prisoner by the Byzantine army. Khalid ibn Walid swiftly took his mobile guard to rescue him. Khawla, knowing her beloved brother was in danger, disguised herself from head to toe in armour, wrapped a green shawl around her waist and chest and veiled her face. She mounted a horse and charged into battle.

She fought so ferociously that soldiers on both sides believed she was Khalid bin Waleed. One of the Rashidun army commanders, Sharjil ibn Hassana, is reported to have said, "This warrior fights like Khalid bin Waleed, but I am sure he is not Khalid."

The Arab Historian, al-Waqidi, narrates in his book "The Conquering of al-Sham [Greater Syria]",

> In a battle that took place in Bayt Lahyah near Ajnadin, Khalid watched a knight in black attire, with a large green shawl wrapped around his waist and covering his chest. That knight broke through the Roman ranks like an arrow. Wondering about the identity of the unknown knight, Khalid and the others followed him and joined battle. Rafe' bin Umayrah al-Ta'if was one of the fighters. He described how that knight scattered the enemy ranks, disappearing in their midst to reappear after a while with blood dripping from his spear. He swerved again and repeated the deed fearlessly, several times. The Muslim army was worried about him and praying for his safety. Rafe' and others thought that he was Khalid, who won great fame for his bravery and genius military plans. But suddenly Khalid appeared with a number of knights. Rafe' asked the leader, "Who is that knight? By God, he has no regard for his safety!"

Khalid answered that he didn't know the man but was in complete awe of his courage. When the Romans finally lost the battle and fled, Khalid looked for the knight and asked him to remove his veil. Khawla was reluctant and tried to withdraw, but after Khalid insisted, the knight said, "I am Khawla bint al-Azwar. I was with the women accompanying the army when I learnt that the enemy captured my brother, which led me to do what I had to do." Khalid ordered his army to chase the fleeing Byzantines with Khawla leading the attack, after which the Muslim prisoners were found and freed.

Khawla bint al-Azwar fought side by side with her brother Dhirar in many battles, including in the decisive Battle of Yarmouk in 636 against the Byzantine Empire. On the fourth day of the battle, she led a group of women against the Byzantine army.

Khawla bint al-Azwar was well known for her leadership in the Muslim conquests in parts of what are known today as Syria, Jordan and Palestine. She was a true warrior who has become a legendary figure to this day. May Allah grant her mercy.

ZUNAIRA AL-RUMIYA

Before becoming a companion of the Prophet ﷺ, Zunaira was a concubine of the Banu Makhzum and a slave-girl of Umar bin al-Khattab.

She was from amongst the first to embrace Islam and after her conversion she was asked to renounce her new religion, but she was committed to her faith and remained steadfast. When Abu Jahl, an enemy of the Prophet ﷺ, heard of her conversion, he beat her so badly that she lost her eyesight. He told her that al-Lāt and al-'Uzzá - the two idols in pre-Islamic Mecca worshipped by the Quraysh - had made her blind because of her disbelief in them. She replied, "And what makes al-lat and al-'Uzza know who is worshipping them? This is from the heavens and my Allah can return my eyesight". The next day her sight was miraculously restored. Abu Bakr ؓ bought her and gave her freedom. May Allah be pleased with Zunaira al-Rumiya, a woman of steadfast faith who gained back her eyes and her freedom.

HAMNA BINT JAHSH

Hamna bint Jahsh was the daughter of Umayma bint Abdul Muttalib, the paternal aunt of the Prophet ﷺ. She was also the sister of Zaynab bint Jahsh, one of the wives of the Prophet ﷺ, and thus she was his cousin as well as his sister-in-law. Hamna became a Muslim in the first years of Islam and was loyal to the Prophet ﷺ with all her heart. She was married to Mus'ab bin Umayr, one of the great Companions, and they led a loving and happy life together.

Mus'ab took part in the battle of Uhud and fought heroically. The Muslims were on the verge of a great big victory but when the archers deserted their places, the course of the battle changed, and the Muslims faced a terrible defeat. A rumour spread that the Prophet ﷺ was martyred.

When Hamna bint Jahsh heard this, she, along with other female Companions in Medina, ran to the battlefront. To their relief, the Messenger of Allah ﷺ was alive, but Hamna was about to receive some painful news. The Prophet ﷺ wanted to give this news to Hamna himself. When she came to him, he said, "O Hamna! Show patience and seek reward from Allah!" Hamna said, "O Messenger of Allah! For whom shall I show patience?" The Prophet ﷺ said, "For your maternal uncle Hamza." She said, "We are slaves of Allah and we will return to Him. May Allah show him mercy and forgive him! May Allah give him glad tidings and rejoice him with the reward of martyrdom!" The Prophet ﷺ said, "O Hamna! Show patience and seek reward from Allah!" Hamna said, "O Messenger of Allah! For whom shall I show patience?" The Prophet said, "For your brother." Hamna said in patience and resoluteness, "We are slaves of Allah and we will return to Him. May Allah show him mercy and forgive him! May Allah give him glad tidings and rejoice him with the reward of martyrdom!"

The Prophet ﷺ said, "O Hamna! Show patience and seek reward from Allah!" Hamna, now fearing the worst, asked, "O Messenger of Allah! For whom shall I show patience?" The Prophet ﷺ said, "For Mus'ab bin Umayr." Hamna's face darkened in grief. She started to weep and exclaim, "Woe upon me!" Thereupon, the Messenger of Allah ﷺ said, "There is no doubt that a man has a different place in the eye of his wife. Hamna showed patience and resoluteness when she heard about the death of her maternal uncle and brother, but she could not maintain her resoluteness when she heard the death of her husband." Hamna was in a well of sadness but found consolation in the Prophet's words ﷺ and submitted to Allah's will.

Hamnah was to find the balm of contentment again when she married Talha bin Ubaydullah, one of the ten Companions who were given the good news that they would be granted Paradise. They shared a happy marriage and were blessed with two children called Muhammad and Imran. May Allah be pleased with Hamna bint Jahsh, a woman with a family of martrys.

www.ingramcontent.com/pod-product-compliance
Lightning Source LLC
Chambersburg PA
CBHW011317080526
44588CB00020B/2735